COPYRIGHT—THE LIBRARIAN AND THE LAW

(Proceedings of the Eighth Annual Symposium sponsored by the Alumni and the Faculty of the Rutgers University Graduate School of Library Service)

GEORGE J. LUKAC, Editor

96

Bureau of Library and Information Science Research
Rutgers University Graduate School of Library Service
New Brunswick, N.J.
1972

Library of Congress Cataloging in Publication Data
Main entry under title:

Copyright—the librarian and the law.

(Issues in the library and information sciences, no. 1)
1. Photocopying processes—Fair use (Copyright)—United States. 2. Copyright—United States. I. Lukac, George J., ed. II. Rutgers University, New Brunswick, N.J. Graduate School of Library Service. III. Series.
KF3030.1.A75C6   346′.73′0482   72-5195
ISBN 0-8135-0746-4

Copyright © 1972

Rutgers University Graduate School of Library Service

Contents

PART I

Issues in the Library and Information Sciences

The Rutgers University Graduate School of Library Service in conjunction with its Bureau of Library and Information Science Research is publishing ISSUES IN THE LIBRARY AND INFORMATION SCIENCES in the hope that it will be relevant, informative, provocative and controversial and will open avenues of information transfer and exchange. We hope the series will provide an avenue for expressing opinions backed by data in an aura of intellectual freedom.

The series will include publications by members of the faculty, by students, by various experts and leaders in the fields, as well as results of particular symposia and meetings that are germane to its purpose.

Henry Voos
Series Editor

Preface

Each spring, the Graduate School of Library Service Alumni Association and the Graduate School of Library Service at Rutgers University jointly sponsor a symposium of interest and importance to librarians. Over the years, these programs have been increasingly well received by those in attendance.

In April, 1970, the symposium was on the topic, "Copyright— The Librarian and the Law." This symposium, the eighth in the series, was so successful, productive and meaningful in its content, particularly in light of the existing problems in the area of copyright and copyright legislation, that the School and the Alumni Association decided that it was virtually imperative to publish the complete proceedings of that day's events. What made the outcome of the eighth annual symposium of special significance was the fact that the five panelists who took part clearly rank among the leading experts in the country today on the subject of copyright. Furthermore, much of the emphasis during the day's discussion was on the subject of photocopying in libraries and on the resultant question of copyright definition with which most librarians are confronted.

Some may question the timing of the publication of this volume in relation to the date of the symposium. As a matter of fact, the proceedings set forth in this book are just as timely and topical now as they were in April, 1970. This is best borne out by a comment made by Barbara A. Ringer, Assistant Register of Copyrights and a participant in the symposium, in a letter to the editor in the spring of 1971. Miss Ringer wrote: "Reading this over gave me a spooky feeling. A whole year has passed and we are exactly where we were on the library photocopying issue. I'll be interested to read your book twenty years from now, to see if we're any further along then." So, it is hoped that this book—the first one ever to emanate from any of the joint symposiums—will make a positive contribution to the continuing discussions on the topic of copyright and particularly library photocopying.

Many people contributed significantly both in arranging and conducting the actual symposium and in the preparation of this book. These individuals should be acknowledged and thanked for their productive efforts. First and foremost, of course, are the five panelists. Not only did they distinguish themselves when they delivered their individual talks and during the afternoon panel discussion, but they all very readily agreed to the publication of their papers and of the transcript of the panel discussion. Moreover, all five devoted many hours of hard work in going over very rough copies of the transcribed texts of what they had said in preparing the copy for publication.

One individual who played a major role in the planning and organizing of the symposium was Mrs. Helen Montgomery, director of the Berkeley Heights, New Jersey, Public Library, who was president of the Alumni Association at the time. Her contribution deserves special recognition. Two members of her library staff also assisted, in particular Mrs. Marjorie Baranoski, who taped the entire proceedings, and Mrs. Kyoko Mukai.

Of course there were those at the Graduate School of Library Service who worked hard in preparing for the symposium, especially Dean Thomas H. Mott. Also assisting was Mrs. Mildred Johnson of the faculty. Among the girls on the staff of Dr. Mott's office, Miss Margaret Koye deserves special thanks for the many hours she put in in preparation for the program, along with the help of other members of the office staff. Mrs. Shirley Bolles, then president-elect of the Alumni Association, also played her part, particularly in presiding at the symposium.

Far from the least of those who contributed was my secretary, Miss Loretta Carneglia, who had much to do both with the symposium and with this book. She not only ably handled considerable detail work in advance of the symposium, but assisted me extensively in many ways in the preparation of the final manuscript.

Last but not least, I must thank my good friend José Carballal, who came to my rescue with very specialized assistance just as the manuscript was reaching completion.

Many people have been active participants in a project which ultimately has led to the publication of this volume. It is my sincere hope that all this work has resulted in a serious contribution to a better understanding of the continuing discussion of a difficult problem—difficult for librarians, authors, publishers and others. If this book accomplishes nothing more, it will at least show where each group in this ongoing dispute stands, and perhaps it may help them move a little closer together. After all, although at times they seem to fail to recognize it, all the elements involved in this controversy really are talking about a common problem.

George J. Lukac
Assistant Director of Alumni Relations

July, 1971

Introduction

The copyright problem is a typical one of economic threat being brought about by changing technology. This technology can be seen as advancing along two fronts. The more general is the development of information transfer by non-print methods using radio, television and, although the final result is usually in printed form, the computer. Interestingly, many librarians join with authors and publishers in feeling threatened by this development. The argument, for such it is, is joined rather over the development of the second front—fast, inexpensive copying devices.

Authors and publishers complain that librarians are operating copying departments which are engaging in activities which are nothing less than piratical publishing, the result being a threat to the economic well-being of authors and publishers. They are disappointed that librarians, who are dependent upon the originality and energy of authors and the fiscal risks of publishers, so callously encourage this. Overlying the fact is the intensity of feeling inherent in any falling-out among old friends.

Librarians particularly resent being accused of sharp practice since most would agree that service to the public is the chief purpose of offering copying facilities. In addition, some libraries subsidize the cost of copying, and even where they do not, overhead costs are seldom fully accounted for. Even more galling is the recollection that many libraries resisted providing copying service until virtually forced to do so by public demand.

In addition to such specific resentments, there are other issues which librarians think entitle them to more understanding treatment. They cite, for example, the recent and sizeable increase in publishing as a result of increased state and federal funding for libraries. In addition there is the development of reprint publishing for which libraries furnish most of the market and usually the original copy as well. They note also that much of the material being copied is scientific for which authors seldom have received royalties and which characteristically have been supported by federal grants.

Meanwhile, attempts to revamp the 1909 copyright law languish in the Congress. Everyone is agreed that the delay is not over the issues noted above, but CATV. Can it be that we are making and listening to the wrong arguments?

Roy L. Kidman
Former Librarian, Rutgers University;
Now Head Librarian, University
    of Southern California

PART II

Our Copyright Law—Present Status and Proposals for Change

Barbara A. Ringer

Miss Ringer is Assistant Register of Copyrights in the Copyright Office of the Library of Congress, Washington, D.C.

The topic I've been asked to speak on—the present status of our copyright law and current proposals for changing it—is something most of you have heard about before. It is a controversial problem and, to use a word someone else used just now, perhaps an insoluble one. To legislative status and proposals, I think I should add some discussion of prospects, even though they are something that I don't think anyone can speak authoritatively about. I will speculate as best I can, and I suspect you will hear some more speculation before the morning is over.

It is no secret to anyone who has read the *A.L.A. Bulletin* or the *Library Journal* or the *Wilson Library Bulletin* that, in the last couple of years, copyright in general and the copyright law revision bill in particular have become matters of urgent concern to the library community. It is accurate to say that the bill for the general revision of the copyright law, which includes a provision bearing directly upon library photocopying, is in a noticeably pregnant state. We are coming toward the end of the Ninety-First Congress, and the bill has been reported by the Senate Subcommittee on Copyright to the full Judiciary Committee. It has been delayed because of the Supreme Court nominations and the voting rights amendment.

However, for reasons I will come to in a moment, the copyright revision bill seems to be hung up on a great deal more than those matters. As I said, the status of the bill is pregnant, but the prognosis for a miscarriage is quite strong. The first question that is being asked is whether the bill is going to go. Secondly, you as librarians would do well to ask: What does it mean to me and my library if it does or if it doesn't go?

To find the answers to these questions, you have to look at what the law is now, and there is a great deal of misunderstanding and misconception on the subject. The present law was written in 1909, has essentially not been changed since 1909 and incorporates provisions that go back into the nineteenth century or even earlier.

The key provision in the present copyright law is section 1, subsection (a), which specifically provides that the copyright owner shall have the exclusive right to print, reprint, publish, copy and vend the copyrighted work. If you take this language literally, it would mean that any person who copies a portion of a copyrighted work by hand would be infringing. Purely as a technical matter, I think this is probably true. But, as someone has said, this provision would be intolerable were it not for a very important concept not stated by the law at present but nevertheless forming a central part of it. That is the concept or doctrine of fair use. Fair use is the rubric under which a great many uses—piecemeal, one-by-one, bit-by-bit uses of copyrighted material—are made. We have audio tape recorders, we are about to see videotape recorders, we have a proliferation of audio and video cassettes and cartridges. And needless to say, we have Xerox and other photocopying machines and the libraries' increasing use of these inventions.

The most important questions now facing a librarian with respect to copyright undoubtedly are these:

How far can I go in allowing unsupervised use of copying machines in a library?

How far can I go in filling orders for photocopies?

How far can I go in replacing deteriorating copies in our collection?

How far can I go in supplying photocopies for inter-library loan?

All these are vitally important issues which will be treated more fully by other speakers. Moreover, what about computers, data systems and information storage as well as retrieval and transfer in general? These are all unanswered questions under the copyright law.

The fact that certain practices have become commonplace doesn't necessarily mean that they are legal. Granted, widespread practices can influence a court's decision; but even if everybody speeds on 46th Street, you may still have to pay a fine if you're caught. A very common misconception, indeed something of an old wives' tale, is the idea that if the use is not for profit it is not an infringement. In other words, you can get away with anything just so long as you are not competing commercially with the copyright owner. This simply isn't true. There is an abundance of cases under the copyright law in which non-profit uses have been held to be infringements. The fact that they were noncompetitive is irrelevant. The motives of the user of the copyright material may well bear on whether or not what he is doing is fair use, but they are not determinative of that issue.

Every case where fair use is raised as a defense must be decided on its merits. This is a very unsatisfactory situation. It is unsatisfactory for the copyright owner, who in some cases finds his property being eroded, and it is unsatisfactory for librarians who want to provide services that their users demand as long as they are legal.

This unsatisfactory tension between fair use and infringement has been with us a long time, but it was not really one of the motivating factors behind the efforts to revise the copyright law. Believe it or not, these efforts date back to 1912. They became very active in 1924, continued on a month-to-month basis up to the Second World War in 1940 and resumed in 1955. Several officials in the Copyright Office, including me, have been spending very large proportions of our time on this since 1955. And in the fifteen years that this large effort has been in germination, we have seen a whole new crop of media for use of copyrighted works grow up. If there is any single reason why the efforts to revise the law may fail, it is the inability of the proposed legislation to cope with the sudden emergence of new media for exploitation and dissemination: computers, photocopying machines and particularly cable television. Although cable television is not exactly a new medium, it did not become a major commercial element until the current revision effort had been under way for nearly a decade. CATV emerged as a major issue in copyright about 1965.

The provisions of the 1909 law that are unsatisfactory in the area of the new media also are unsatisfactory in practically every other area. There are a host of technical difficulties, and there are substantive difficulties arising from the structure of the statute. There are a number of things that seem to say one thing on paper and mean something else in practice. Such a word as "publication," for example, has six or eight different senses in different sections of the law. The statute was enacted at the beginning of the twentieth century, but the theories on which it is based are nineteenth century theories. It was not a twentieth century law, and we are now faced with twenty-first century problems under a nineteenth century law.

I can say from excruciating personal experience that this seems like Alice in Wonderland to the Europeans. Our law derives from a statute that was enacted under Queen Anne in 1710, and that in turn was based on premises going back to Shakespearean times and before. We have carried a whole accretion of common law and ancient principles into a situation that cries out for new thinking and efficient legal solutions. Since the Second World War we have emerged as the foremost exporter of literary material in the world, but our laws are completely different from any other copyright laws in the world. One important example is that in fixing the duration of copyright, we are still stuck with the unrealistic concept of "publication" and have not adopted a term based on the life of the author which is in effect in practically every other country in the world. This just seems incredible to the Europeans.

For a number of years the program for general revision of the copyright law showed increasing signs of success, and we were making visible progress in Congress. It looked as if we were finally going to get ourselves into a position where our law was compatible with that of other countries. The fact that we now may be doomed to failure is going to be very difficult to explain abroad. I know that those in other countries are going to be saying, "Oh, those Americans—they have been fooling us all along. What they really want to do is continue to take our works and not pay for them, while we have to pay for all their works we take."

Why has the present program failed? To put it glibly, the answer consists of four letters: CATV. When the bill reached the House floor in April, 1967, it had only two major unresolved issues: cable television, which had just emerged as a major issue, and jukeboxes. A good example of why the 1909 law is outdated is that it completely exempts jukebox performances from copyright liability. Muzak has to pay, local broadcasters have to pay, but a jukebox doesn't have to pay anything for music performances. The bill was debated all day on Thursday, April 6, 1967, and very nearly came to a sudden death at that point because of these two issues and the interplay between them. The jukebox issue was resolved by a compromise. It wasn't a perfect compromise, but it has shown signs of sticking in the years since 1967.

The CATV issue was too big and complex to be compromised, and the result was that it was simply knocked out of the bill. Nobody quite knew what that meant, but the obvious feeling was that the other House would have to cope with it. Unfortunately, the Senate has not been able to cope with it. There are a variety of reasons for this. I don't think that anyone is to blame, and I don't think that any one interest group can be pointed at as the villain in what was a piece of bad luck of timing. But we do have a major issue which has been unresolvable up to this time, and unless there is some sort of resolution I don't think the bill is going to go.

Thus, to answer my first question, I think the bill is going to go only if the CATV issue is resolved one way or the other. This is not necessarily apparent to people like librarians who have other and very different interests in the copyright law.

On Tuesday, April 11, following that memorable Thursday, the amended bill was passed by the House of Representatives by a large, one-sided vote. Thereafter, the library organizations, which previously had been content to leave things as they were, gradually began to get concerned with the provisions of the bill. After literally five or more years in which librarians had been quiet on copyright revision, they came forward with a proposal that the publishers and authors were not prepared to accept. There ensued a number of months of discussion. There were a variety of issues, but they essentially boiled down to library photocopying: the use of the machines and the extent to which the library could make copies on order for readers or other libraries.

The negotiations looked very promising for a time. I think this was an illusion, and, looking back on it, I realize that what we had here was a failure to communicate. The communication may not be perfect now, but I think that the issues are a little clearer. I think that both sides have moved a little. Neither side is well served by the present law. If the library community and the publishing community continue indefinitely into the future with the 1909 law, which leaves these questions unanswered, there is sure to be more litigation and a great deal of uncertainty. I don't think anyone's interest is served by this.

What I am going to say now is not a prognosis; it's a hope. I would hope that whatever happens to the copyright revision bill, there will be a genuine constructive effort on both sides, as there has been in the past, to try to resolve this problem through legislation. Legislation in this area is badly needed. I believe there is a willingness to concede certain things on both sides and a willingness to negotiate on other things that have not yet produced agreement. It is worth a good hard try. If the bill doesn't go this year, I think those people in the organizations representing both sides would do well to try to come together and work out some sort of legislative program.

What is now before Congress apparently is not acceptable to the librarians, and I will leave it to other speakers to explain why. In its present form, the bill assumes that there would be no control over unsupervised copying machines. If all we are talking about is copying actually supervised or conducted by the library, then the library representatives would like to see a line drawn between single and multiple copies; multiple copying would be regarded as an infringement, but a single copy would be permitted.

This remains an unresolved issue. There has been a good

deal of discussion on this point, and on the basis of it I believe the publishers and authors are unwilling to concede unlimited single copying. The librarians on their side are willing to concede that "single copying" is really making a single copy and is not just one-by-one multiple copying. When you have a book on the reserve shelf in a college library and you have fifty students coming in and each one ordering a copy of the same three chapters, this is not single copying. I think the librarians are willing to concede copyright control in the situation where it is not spontaneous but is really the concerted copying by various users of single works. What they are not willing to concede is that there would be a line drawn within the works, that it would be a reasonable portion of a work—one article in a periodical, for example. I think there is room for negotiation here.

I want to say one further word about the computer issue and its relevance to this problem. Like the library photocopying issue, the issue of computer input and use of copyrighted material arose after the House hearings and after much of the shouting had already been done in the professional arena. The difference between library photocopying and computer input is not that the law is any clearer on one than on the other. It is, rather, that computer input has not yet gotten off the ground, and therefore the computer people are not bargaining from a fixed position. They are not already doing it; it is something they want to do in the future. Because of this, an agreement was reached to the effect that, since Congress does not have the data on which to base detailed legislation with respect to computer input and transfer of information of copyrighted material, it should create a legislative commission which would study the problem and report the results to Congress. Only then would Congress act.

There is a provision in the bill now before the Senate Judiciary Committee to the effect that, with respect to information storage, retrieval and transfer, whatever the law was on the day before the new law comes into effect stays the law. This sort of provision is not a very good legislative solution to this or anything else, but it was something that people could agree upon. The copyright interests were willing to say: "Okay, librarians and academics, go ahead and experiment with computer input. We won't sue you. Meanwhile, we, the publishers and authors, are not giving away our rights. And pardon our stopgap expediency.''

What I am afraid of is that the bill will begin to crumble when it becomes obvious that it would be passed this year. I reiterate: for reasons of CATV, we are running out of time in Congress. The disintegration of the package, if it comes, is going to produce a lot of little separate issues that are going to continue kicking around. It would be very convenient for Congress to throw all of this into the commission. The commission could then balloon into another study of copyright law revision, which conceivably could go on for another fifteen years, just as ours has, and with just about the same result.

I would strongly urge resistance to any efforts aimed at pushing all these issues under the commission rug. If the package will not budge, the issues should be confronted separately, but they should be confronted now and not shoved aside. I realize the picture I have painted is not a very bright one, but the prospect of deferring solutions to these problems for another generation or more seems to me considerably bleaker.

Library Photocopying—The Publisher's View

Charles H. Lieb

Mr. Lieb is senior partner in the New York law firm of Paskus, Gordon & Hyman and is a director and counsel of John Wiley & Sons, Inc. He is copyright counsel to the Association of American Publishers and chairman of the American Bar Association Copyright Division for 1971–72.

Library photocopying presented a copyright problem forty years ago through the general use of photostating equipment. Today, with the advent of xerography and because high speed duplicators are available in every library, the problem has been compounded many times. Worse still, where there was a common understanding of the problem and at least partial agreement in principle before, there appears to be very little agreement now. While it is understandable that tempers fray as pressures increase, it should be possible for publishers and librarians, members alike of the scholarly community, to reach a reasoned solution. With Tallyrand's advice in mind, "above all, no zeal," let us try to review the issues which divide us and find a solution.

First, to examine the position of the librarian and the publisher. The research librarian considers it his function today to offer on-the-premises copying facilities to student and researcher. Unless he does so, Verner Clapp has said, he cannot pretend to serve serious study and must restrict himself to recreational readers.

The publisher is not so foolish to challenge this. He knows that photocopying is here to stay and that rapid and inexpensive transmission of photocopies by cable and satellite is around the corner. The publisher does not resist library photocopying; he urges rather that the user of the photocopy bear his fair share of the cost of creating the work, or, at the very least, make good the income that otherwise would be lost to the publisher because of the use of the photocopy rather than the original.

This is of concern not only to the private sector publisher, who can attract capital only if his books return a profit, but to the not-for-profit university presses and the journal-publishing professional societies as well. The American Chemical Society, for example, has stated its deep concern that unauthorized photocopying from its journals and abstracts may impair or even destroy its ability to generate and publish scientific information. The Association of American University Presses, in its Resolution on Permissions, makes clear for the same reason that copying beyond citation of authority or for criticism or review requires specific consent and, in appropriate cases, payment.

What impels the publisher, whether a John Wiley, a professional society or a university press to protect the expected income from the sale of its published work is the inexorable rule that if income from sales or from other rights is less than outgo for the cost of production and the cost of the required capital, publishing will become uneconomic and, therefore, not possible except as subsidized or fully supported by government. It is perhaps not too melodramatic to suggest that if that day should come, there will be little left of freedom of the press as we know it now.

I am aware of the librarian's scepticism that photocopying does in fact diminish the publisher's revenues. Scepticism or no, the ability of the photocopying machine to produce single copies at small cost must necessarily affect the market for published material. The real question is not *whether* photocopying done by librarians affects the publisher's market but the *extent* to which the photocopies supplied by the librarian reduce the expected income from the book.

The answer is not clear. Studies in the past, although helpful, have of necessity been superficial and have not even touched upon the effect which library photocopying will have upon sales of the photocopied work when high speed cable or microwave transmission of photocopies becomes economically more feasible. One journal publisher feels so strongly that it is presently being copied to death that it has brought suit against the government, which, through the National Institutes of Health Library and the National Library of Medicine, has been circulating photocopies of its journal articles.

I am aware, too, that many librarians feel that, at most,

library photocopying merely reduces the "additional profit" which the publisher unfairly seeks for the lawful use of the book which the librarian has already bought and paid for.

There are two points here rolled into one which require answer. First, as to the profiteering. I have no direct knowledge of the profitability of best-selling fiction, but I can tell you that profits from the sale of technical and reference works with which research librarians are primarily concerned are modest and that, such as they are, they are shared in about equal proportions with the author as royalties.

As for the second point—that the purchase of the book carries with it the right to make photocopies of it for the use of others—it overlooks the essential nature of copyright, namely, that although the purchaser may sell or lend the book or give it away, he may not make copies of it beyond the limits of fair use. This has been so since the very beginnings of copyright. It is no more true that because a book has been purchased its contents may be copied and distributed than that the patented photocopying machine itself that has been purchased may be copied and reproduced for distribution.

The copyright proprietor by statute has the exclusive right to print, reprint, publish, copy and vend the copyrighted work. That right, nevertheless, is subject to the right of others to make "fair use" of the work. The fair use doctrine is an equitable rule of reason. John Schulman has likened it to the golden rule—that one should not copy from someone else what he would not want copied from himself. Its application depends on the facts. Broadly speaking, the criteria by which fair use is determined are the purpose of the use, the nature of the copyrighted work, the quantity and value of the materials used and the degree in which the use may prejudice the sale or diminish the profits or supersede the objects of the original work.

Librarians complain of uncertainty because of the generality of the fair use concept. I don't understand this concern. As far as I know, no librarian has ever been hailed into court because of misjudgment of the limits of fair use. What is more, the concept of fair use is no more intangible than that of negligence or reasonable care or other doctrines which depend for their application upon the facts of the particular case and with which we live quite comfortably in our daily lives.

Fair use was the basis for the "Gentleman's Agreement" of 1935 between research librarians and publishers. In that agreement, the parties, recognizing that it would be unfair if libraries should substitute a photostat for the purchase of the book itself, agreed not to supply photocopies exceeding the limits of fair use.

Fair use is the basis of the Association of American University Presses' Resolution on Permissions to which I referred before. That resolution recognizes the obligation of the scholar "to avoid quoting in such amounts, over and beyond scholarly needs, as to impair or destroy the property rights and financial benefits of their fellow scholars and the original publishers from whose work they are quoting."

That fifty-five universities subscribe to this resolution illustrates what Arpena Mesrobian, in her article in the January, 1970, issue of *Scholarly Publishing,* describes as the complexities arising out of the dual and sometimes contradictory nature of university press publishing. As one who seeks permission to reprint materials belonging to someone else, the author seeks the greatest possible latitude in their use. But once his book has been published, he quite rightly expects that his publisher will protect the editorial integrity as well as the financial value of the literary property in which they share interest. The university press on the one hand, she says, is dedicated to the advancement of scholarship but, on the other, to its legal and moral commitment to the publishing enterprise and the literary property entrusted to its care.

University presses are no different from private sector publishers in this respect, nor is there any difference in principle between the photocopying which we talk about today and the reprinting which Miss Mesrobian discusses.

For many years, the library world leaned heavily on the Gentleman's Agreement to justify its photocopying services. Presumably, that means that in the main, library photocopying was restricted to fair use. However, the agreement is now a dead letter. Librarians became dissatisfied with it, and the successors to the signing publishers' organization never ratified it.

The agreement, in today's light, is clearly deficient in several respects. It is deficient from the library's point of view because it did not recognize the library's justified need to reproduce an out-of-print work not available through authorized reproducing sources. It is deficient from the publisher's point of view because it did not foresee the publisher's need to be protected against the multiple copying that is possible today with high-speed copying machines.

Where does that leave us then? The librarian considers photocopying a necessary extension of his service. He knows or should know that he may photocopy only within the limits of fair use. He is not certain of just what latitude that allows him. He is certain, however, that it will not permit him to photocopy everything his patron may request.

Is this a desirable situation? Let us agree that it is not. Let us accept that in given instances the student, the researcher or even the casual reader should be able to obtain from the library portions of copyrighted works in excess of fair use in place of the published work itself.

But the question remains, in what manner? By so diluting copyright protection that any work may be copied to any extent without compensation to the proprietor? I think not. This is hardly the way to preserve an independent publishing industry. The effort, instead, should be to clarify to the extent possible the line that separates copying which may be done without permission from that which requires permission and to establish a means by which permission, when required, can be quickly obtained.

Three sections of the copyright revision bill now before the Senate attempt to clarify what may be copied without permission.

Section 107 would, for the first time, establish fair use as a statutory right.

Section 504 would relieve the librarian of liability for statutory damages for an unintentional infringement resulting from photocopying beyond fair use.

Section 108, which made its first appearance in the December, 1969, committee print and which deals specifically with libraries and archives by guaranteeing to libraries all photocopying rights they now have and by extending additional photocopying rights would for the first time draw a statutory line between permissible and improper photocopying.

Section 108 deserves close attention. The section first defines the institutions which are to receive its benefit. These are libraries and archives and their employees, provided that the photocopying is done on a noncommercial basis and that the collections of the library or archives are open to the public.

The section establishes the right of the library to photocopy a work for itself or for another library for replacement purposes if an unused replacement cannot be obtained through normal trade channels or authorized reproducing services. This, in my view, is a new right and not fair use as we know it now.

The section also establishes a library right to make a photocopy of a work for its patron if an unused copy cannot be obtained through normal trade sources or authorized reproducing services. This is also a new right.

The foregoing rights apply to out-of-print works.

The section, in addition, gives specific recognition to the library's right to make photocopies of works in print within the limits of fair use. This would allay any existing doubt that fair use can justify a library to make a copy not for its own use but for the use of its patron. I understand that some librarians read the section differently, construing it instead as a limitation of the library's present right to rely on fair use. I believe they are mistaken. Subsection (E) (3) specifically provides that nothing in section 108 "in any way affects the right of fair use as provided by section 107." The purpose of the draftsmen clearly is to assure to libraries the full benefit of fair use, and I would expect that this will be stated in so many words in the legislative report.

The section would also remove the liability the librarian might otherwise incur for allowing the unsupervised use of photocopying equipment on the library premises.

Section 108 makes clear, however, that the granted photocopying rights apply only to the isolated and unrelated reproduction of a single copy on separate occasions and not to the related or concerted reproduction of multiple copies whether on one occasion or over a period of time and whether intended for aggregate use by one individual or for separate use by the individual members of a group. This is primarily to protect the publisher against multiple copying of textbooks or of other required course reading by a college library, a practice which publishers and authors regard as tantamount to piratical reprinting.

The library associations have proposed an amendment to the section which would permit photocopying—of a work in print—for distribution to a patron upon the patron's certification that he will use the copy in accordance with the fair use provisions of Section 107. But when before has the fox's assurance of good intentions given him free entry into the chicken coop? Where the photocopied extract and the use that is made of it are in fact within the limits of fair use, the amendment would give no right not already granted and would be redundant. But where the copying or the use exceeds the fair use privilege, as will frequently be the case, it will by that very fact detract from the financial value of the copied work and undermine the economic basis upon which the publication of books must depend. The proposed amendment, by condoning and indeed encouraging infringement, would go far in destroying the entire fabric of copyright protection.

You may feel that I am exaggerating and that an occasional copying beyond fair use will harm neither author nor publisher. But this assumes that the copying would be occasional and overlooks the tremendous impairment in value of the copyrighted work which would result if the copying, even if occasional at one library, were repeated in the same occasional manner at scores of other libraries.

The revision bill represents progress. By the very nature of copyright, however, it cannot satisfy the librarian's desire to provide photocopies of a work in print in excess of fair use. Here the answer lies not in destruction of copyright rights but in the creation of procedures acceptable to publisher and librarian which will permit the making of the desired copies.

The establishment of a clearing house for this purpose has frequently been discussed. But a clearing house would be costly, and librarians have said that the responsibility for establishing it should rest with the publishers. And publishers have replied that if the librarians need a clearing house they should establish it themselves. Partisan and one-sided positions such as these are of no help. If a clearing house was otherwise practicable, I would think that its financing might be supplied by government or by government-supported foundations.

There is much doubt, however, that a clearing house with its attendant complexity and high installation and operating costs is really needed. Certainly an ASCAP* or BMI** type organization would not be useful because of the inherent differences between literary material and music.

Perhaps a copyright information center on the order of the organization just recently established under the aegis of Franklin Book Programs to assist in the clearance of publishing rights for developing countries might be of help. Or perhaps an effort by libraries through their associations to bargain with publishers for overall copying rights might create a satisfactory modus vivendi.

I do not pretend to know the solution to this perplexing problem. I do strongly believe, however, that the necessary accommodation between publisher and librarian will be found only by strenuous good faith efforts by all parties.

I see no reason why the principles that should govern library photocopying in excess of fair use should not be agreed upon by the parties directly involved. There have been many studies and surveys made in the past, but they have been made either solely by librarians or solely by publishers or by third parties. To the best of my knowledge, librarians and publishers have not, since 1935, joined in a cooperative effort to survey and resolve their common problem to their own satisfaction.

I think it is time that the chasm is bridged and that librarians and publishers organize a joint study group to examine all open questions with respect to library photocopying and to outline practicable solutions. Because the problems arise differently for so many different kinds of published works, I would suggest that as a first step the study group confine itself to the photocopying of technical and scientific books and journals by research librarians. If the problems in this area of publishing can be solved in this manner, it should

*American Society of Composers, Authors and Publishers
**Broadcast Music, Inc.

not be difficult to arrive at appropriate solutions in other areas of publishing.

The study group approach has produced constructive results in other fields at other times, and there is no reason why it should not be productive now. I do not offer it as a perfect solution, but it would be, I think, a pragmatic response to a difficult problem that becomes increasingly difficult as technology advances.

Copyright—The Author's View

Irwin Karp

Mr. Karp is a partner in the New York law firm of Hays, St. John, Abramson & Heilbron and is attorney for the Author's League of America.

In 1969, at about this time, Jerome Weidman, who is president of the Author's League, spoke at a rally on the steps of the New York Public Library on 42nd Street. Along with several other authors and other New Yorkers, he pleaded for funds from the city and state to keep the library operating at full capacity. It wasn't a particularly historic moment, but it had ironic overtones. Because if the New York Public Library gets all the money it asks for, and I hope it does, and if it gets the amendment to the copyright law which the library representatives are after, the printing factory on the third floor of the library is going to be able to turn out a copy of Mr. Weidman's new book for anybody who comes along and asks for it. And Mr. Weidman isn't going to get a penny despite all that money that he is asking the city and state to give to the New York Public Library.

As the *New York Post* reported in November of 1969, at the New York Public Library headquarters on 42nd Street, "Copying is a big business, transacted in the central room on the third floor where eighty workers man more than thirty duplicators." Our problem is not just the ten-cent copy and it is not just the New York Public Library. And our problem probably doesn't involve most of you in a sense at all. What our problem is concerned with—and when I say ours, I speak of authors—is the fact that copying, done on the New York Library branch scale or the National Institutes of Health branch scale or on a more modest scale, on the new machines that are available, will permit libraries, universities and institutions to function as a new medium of reprint publishing. This will inflict serious injury on authors, on publishers, ultimately on the public and on you, a profession dedicated to serving the public.

The issue created by photocopying and copyright is not whether libraries should be prevented from making copies on order for their patrons. The issue, rather, is: What happens when these copies exceed the limits of fair use and also exceed the new privilege—and I emphasize new privilege—that libraries would have if the present bill were passed? When those limits are exceeded the issue is: Should the author be paid? Bluntly and plainly, what library representatives are fighting for in Congress today is simply one principle—that an author should not be paid no matter how extensive the copy is which is made of his work by a library on a copying machine when a patron requests a copy. That's what their amendment boils down to, and I will go into more detail shortly.

The issue is not whether librarians should pay. No one has ever asked the librarian to pay for anything. Nor have the library representatives who speak for your organizations in Congress been asked. Here we are fighting over the question of whether somebody else should pay for using the author's property. It's as simple as that—whether the public which provides the funds to libraries should provide a small portion of them to pay royalties to the author. Or in the case of a private institution, which runs the gamut from Dupont Research libraries on down to historical archives, whether the private institution should pay when its copying machines make a copy that exceeds fair use.

Let me go back and consider briefly for you the author's view of the copyright revision bill. When an author writes a manuscript, he creates something which is now his absolute property in common law. Nobody can copy it, and nobody can publish it. As long as he chooses to hold it, it is his, and it passes on to his children, his grandchildren and to other generations and posterity. In fact, one of the most important revisions the bill makes is to end this system of common law copyright. If the bill were passed, no librarian or archivist would ever have to worry again about whether he could allow somebody to make or whether he himself could make copies of Jefferson's letters or Lincoln's manuscripts. Because fifty years after the death of any individual, anything he ever wrote would go into the public domain.

Yet some educational representatives have told Congressmen that this provision is a grab by authors for additional rights at the public expense. This is utter nonsense. It is a reform which will probably be much more beneficial to historians, archivist, librarians and others than it is to most authors living today. But over the last ten years, there has been a barrage of criticism over this provision. Anyone wishing to discuss this further may do so during the symposium panel.

Once any literary work is published, the author must exchange what is absolute common law copyright for a limited period of protection under the United States Copyright Act. He has protection for twenty-eight years, and then he can renew for another twenty-eight years. After that, what he has written goes into the public domain.

Copyright is a unique form of property, because, unlike anything else, it starts in the most private domain—a person's mind—and, at the end of fifty-six years, the government takes it away from him. Most other property, including the land we stand on, oil, coal or any natural resource, starts in the public domain. The government, by an act of Congress, takes it away from the public and hands it over to Standard Oil Company or the individual who receives a land grant of public acreage. It then remains private property forever and ever. Copyright is quite unique because it comes out of the private domain into the public domain by an act of Congress, whereas most other property, by act of Congress, travels in just the opposite direction. It is not, I might note for the record, because copyright is a so-called "monopoly." It is not a "monopoly" in the anti-trust sense; to characterize it as such is untrue from the legal point of view. Copyright is only a "monopoly" in the sense that *all* other private property is—no one can use it without the owner's consent. And it is not like a patent. It bears no resemblance to a patent.

I say this because classroom teachers and others who know nothing about copyright law at this late date are still responding to form letters telling them that copyrights are like patents and the authors of America are trying to put something over on them by having Congress pass a law which would give their works protection for life plus fifty years. This—or a longer term—happens to be the term of copyright law in every civilized country in the world except this one and the Soviet Union.

What are the limitations on copyright? First, let me address myself to the particular rights which the copyright act gives authors. In Section 1, as Miss Ringer says, the author is granted a series of exclusive rights in his work—the right to record it, the right to perform it, the right to read it for profit. But for many authors, the most important right in the copyright act is the right to make copies of his work, because that is how he makes his income. Many book authors earn little or no other income from any other use of their works. The right to make copies is not limited to the copying of an entire work. It also includes the right to copy a substantial portion, anything that exceeds fair use. This, too, has a tremendous economic importance to authors, because many derive a substantial part of their income from granting the right to make copies of excerpts from a work or making copies of shorter self-contained works like articles, poems and short stories.

The copyright revision bill does not expand the author's copying rights one iota. It gives the author nothing new that he does not have now. In fact it takes away quite a bit, to the benefit of librarians and institutes. I think this point should be stressed, because a lot of the propaganda put forth in the last fifteen years has pretty much obscured this fact. It has been said that book authors somehow are getting a great big windfall out of the copyright revision bill, and this is simply not so. Composers of music would derive substantial benefit, because, for the first time, they would be paid when their records were used by commercial interests that operate jukeboxes. They haven't been paid in the last sixty years for this use, while in most countries they are. And composers of music would also get a higher statutory royalty when their records are recorded without their consent, under a compulsory license provision of the copyright law at present. As far as the author of a book, short story or poem is concerned, nothing is added to what he now has and much is taken away. This is not an author's bill, and anybody who knows his copyright law and analyzes the bill closely will tell you the same thing; all the author gets out of this bill is a longer term of copyright.

And this only helps those whose works are valuable enough to survive for the fifty-year period beyond their lifetime.

Authors also benefit from the elimination of something called the manufacturing clause, which, it is universally agreed, is a harsh and unfair provision throwing an American author's work into the public domain if it is published in a foreign country and is not published here in five years.

Fair use, as Miss Ringer and Mr. Lieb have told you, is the principle exception to this copying right. Since it has already been discussed by them, I shall not go into it further.

How do we stand then in the copyright revision situation? We have a law. And I should defend the present law because I think Miss Ringer treats it too harshly. Actually the present law and the new law are not too different in terms of rights they grant authors. They are pretty much the same with some improvement, as I have indicated, for composers concerning the jukebox use of music. Criticism that the present law is vaguely worded is not really too fair, because we have a system of jurisprudence quite different from other countries.

For example, the Sherman Act simply says that a combination, contract or conspiracy in restraint of trade is illegal. That's the whole of Section 1 of the Sherman Act; and Section 2 only says an attempt to monopolize or a monopoly are illegal. Yet, based on these sparse provisions, a whole body of law has been built up by the courts of the United States regulating anti-trust violations and the creation of monopolies. I believe the courts did a better job than Congress would have done if the task had been left to Congress. All of us, as consumers, would have suffered grossly and grievously had we written a European-size detailed statute. In Europe, as a matter of fact, there is no protection against monopoly or restraints of trade in most countries.

The copyright law actually was well written in the sense that, although it was composed in 1909 before modern technology developed—radio, television and motion pictures—it was broad enough so that an author's rights were protected in all these media under the language of Section 1. And the protection won't change much under the new bill. The bill makes several technical changes, but, even there, some of those weren't really needed.

The revision bill does change considerably some of the rights that authors now have to control the copying of their work. For example, in Section 108, librarians are given the right to make a copy of any unpublished manuscript for archival purposes or study and to deposit copies in other libraries. This they can't do under the present copyright act, because it doesn't even control this activity. It is prohibited by the common law which, as I told you, gives the author the absolute property right over any unpublished manuscript. This means that any paper of Mark Twain's, a manuscript such as *Letters to the Earth* which he wrote back in the beginning of this century, could not be copied by anyone. Only when his executors in 1968 chose to publish the manuscript did it come under the federal act, and then it was protected for another fifty-six years. This would all be done away with if the revision bill passed. Anything that Twain ever wrote would go into the public domain here, fifty years after his death, which would have been in 1960, just as it goes into the public domain in every other country of the world. Now that is a change of tremendous importance to people other than authors.

Secondly, Section 108 would give libraries the right—which they do not have now—to make a copy of any complete work to replace a damaged copy if they can't buy one from trade sources at normal prices. The section would also eliminate all question about a library's liability or responsibility for copying on coin-operated machines. It says the library is not responsible. That issue is far from clear under the present law.

Lastly, and this is the only problem we have with library representatives, there is a provision dealing with the library's rights to make copies for its patrons. I use the euphemistic word "patrons," because when I say customers, some legislative representatives of the library associations rankle. But these users are customers. They are putting money on the counter to get something. And it is in this area that we are having problems, only in this area.

Our problem is that library representatives have asked for an amendment to the present revision bill which would literally give any library the right to make a copy of any copyrighted work and deliver it free of charge or for a fee to anyone who ordered it. The so-called limitation on this practice proposed by the library representatives is no limitation at all. They propose that the user need only certify that he will use the copy in accordance with Section 107, which, in common language, means that the customer says, "I certify that I will use this copy for the purpose of fair use."

Now that is utter nonsense. Every copy of a book that is bought at a book store is used by the customer in a manner that constitutes fair use. He takes it home and reads it, puts it on the shelf; he refers to it, enjoys it or learns from it or studies it. That's not the problem. The problem is that if he went to the book store and said, "I am going to use the book for fair use," and the book seller said, "Fine, why bother to pay the publisher a royalty; here I'll run off a copy for you," the author could sue for infringement—and win. The ultimate use of copies by a customer—of a library or book store—is a fair use. It is the making of the copy that's the problem. That's where the author makes his living, and the change proposed by the library representatives would seriously affect his present right to do so.

What is photocopying? What is a copy? Appearing before the House Judiciary Committee, one of your former distinguished representatives held up a pencil and said, "This is a copying instrument, and the Xerox machine is a copying instrument. There's no difference between them." From this thinking we come to our present impasse. The copy I hold in my left hand is a printed copy of a book; the copy I hold in my right hand is a Xerox copy of the same book. They are both printed copies. What you get out of a Xerox machine is a printed page. In a common-sense sense, it's a printing machine.

What we are talking about is what Mr. Powers, president of University Microfilms, once described as the full circle that we have turned in the technology of communication. He said, "We have gone a full circle from the manuscript book to the monk in the monastery copying out in longhand to the small edition of the early printing press to the large edition of modern printing presses back to the small edition of ordinary offset printing and now back to the single copy produced on demand." As I said, one of these copies, and you couldn't tell which, came off a Xerox copying machine, and the other came off a printing press.

The next argument that we have to cope with in this debate of fifteen years duration is whether copying is harmful to authors. I'll forget about publishers; let them speak for themselves. I'm concerned with authors. The fact of the matter is that many authors make a good deal of their living not from the royalties from the trade edition of a book, but from granting to other people permissions to make copies of part of their work. It is obvious that the copying of an entire book can hurt if it is done without permission and without payment. What is not so obvious is that the copying of a part of a work can hurt. As I say, many authors make a living or a good part of a living by granting permission to others to make copies of part of a work. A poet, for example, can make as much as seventy-five percent of his income from granting reprint permissions to use particular poems on a non-exclusive basis in anthologies—that is, to allow the making of a lot of copies of one poem, which are then bound up and sold along with a lot of copies of a lot of other pieces of work.

Eudora Welty just published a novel. In the several years that have elapsed since the publication of her two books of short stories, she has made more money from granting permission to reprint individual stories than she ever made on the original sale of the trade edition of this book. Even novelists like John Dos Passos, a great and respected creator in the halls of American literature, testified before the United States Senate that he made as much as twenty to twenty-five percent of his living by granting permissions to reprint chapters and excerpts of his books in anthologies.

Anthology publishing, as some of you may know, has also been revolutionized by the new technology because now some publishers are even selling individual pieces of work. Bobbs Merrill, for example, sells articles of all sorts by the single article on any number of subjects. Bobbs Merrill and the author get the royalties for that single copy of that single work. Simon and Schuster will put together, on order from a college professor, an anthology for classes in editions as small as 100 to 200 copies containing any articles he chooses. And the authors receive a royalty. That is licensed copying.

Now it doesn't stretch the imagination too much to realize that the same type of copying with the same effect can be done by an institution on the Xerox machine or the photocopying machine. The same article that you can buy from Bobbs Merrill the student can have the library run off for him on the Xerox machine, and the effect is the same. The same short story that Miss Welty could make money from by giving permission to Macmillan to reprint copies in an anthology sold to universities, a university could have for its students if its library has the right to make copies for anybody who wanted them. Much has been made of the fact that no one wants to make multiple copies; it is only single copying that librarians are asking for. But that's an Alice in Wonderland analysis. If you make forty copies at the same time and give them to forty people as they order them, or if each of the forty people come in and have one copy made to order, you would have forty people with forty copies. What difference does it make if you make the forty copies once or if you make them one at a time? That's what the Xerox machine is all about; it makes copies one at a time. And that's how people buy books, one at a time. So this talk about single copying versus multiple copying is pretty much clouding the issue.

Now the last thing I wanted to discuss is the point that this is all theoretical. Who is going to spend money copying a book, a chapter or a short story on a Xerox machine when it is available in print? Let me tell you that the amendment that is proposed by the copyright bill takes account of all that, and your representatives have rejected it because the copyright revision bill would permit the copying of a work for use only if a copy wasn't available through normal trade sources at a reasonable price. Your representatives rejected that. They asked for an amendment which would permit copying to be done even though copies were available through trade sources at a normal price.

What about price? First of all, according to the Xerox Corporation as of yesterday, the 914 produces seven copies a minute at a cost of five cents a copy. The 813, which is a table top, eleven copies a minute, four cents a copy; the 660, eleven copies a minute, 4-1/2 cents a copy; the 720, twelve copies a minute, three cents a copy; the 3600, one to twenty copies, .9 of a cent, and twenty to forty copies even cheaper; the 7000 goes down to as little as .21 cents for a copy. And that is nothing, because we are talking about technology that has exploded in ten years. We don't know how far it will go, how cheap it will be. We are talking about writing into the copyright law today an exemption, or some people are, that would permit this type of copying on the assumption that the cost is a natural prohibitive factor. In fact it isn't prohibitive right now, and in a few years the cost will be so cheap that no one can assume logically it will inhibit copying.

The fact of the matter is if you buy a book of James Dickey's poetry, you are getting fifty pages for $4.50. At even five cents a page you can copy the book cheaper than you can buy it. If a library can do that, if that printing factory on 42nd Street can do it to order, every college kid that wants to read James Dickey is going to be up there instead of going into a book store and paying twice as much.

Now I missed an opportunity when the House Judiciary Committee asked a question about binding. The Xerox copy of the book I showed you is sold commercially. How are they bound? By something called a stapling machine. It's like the magazines you and I purchase. Technically, there are no obstacles to copying on machines replacing the printing press. What it all comes down to is a concept of property and its affect on creativity. Chekhov once said, when you command "forward," be sure to specify which direction you mean, because if you yell forward to a revolutionary and a monk, they will take off in opposite directions.

Now "forward" to me does not mean taking this basic right away from the author. As we sit here close to the New Jersey Turnpike, fortunately not close enough to be affected by the fumes, those of us who live in New York, Newark or Washington and watch the city suffocate and strangle by virtue of the "progress" made in building gasoline engines and roads know by now that ecologically, "progress" can mean different things, including disaster. It is not "progress" to just take any piece of machinery that somebody invented, use it to the bitter end and not pay attention to social effects of that use. We have proven to ourselves that we can destroy our environment, choke ourselves to death in the process in many other areas.

In talking about copyright, we are speaking of a system under which American authors and other authors throughout the world survive professionally and create. They do it under a system of private property rights. They get paid for what they create, and their payment comes in royalties eked out (over a long period of time, in many cases) from each copy sold and for each new use that can be made of the work. It is a lot of nonsense to argue that one new technology doesn't replace another and therefore the author isn't entitled to something when his works are copied on the new machines. First of all, there will be a lot of replacement—loss of sales of conventional books. Secondly, the paperback book ultimately did not replace the hard cover trade edition, but I never heard anybody say that the paperback publisher should be entitled to publish his edition without paying royalties to the author because his edition wasn't displacing the sale of hard cover editions.

Under the system of private entrepreneurial authorship, the author is entitled to something when Xerox copies of his work, exceeding fair use, are produced. When library customers put down their dollars for copies, they are not paying for several pieces of Xerox paper. They are paying money to get something that somebody else wrote, just like they pay on a book store counter. We are not suggesting that they pay for every copy, because fair use actually covers much of the copying that is done for scholarly and educational research purposes. What we are suggesting—when the copying gets beyond that—is not that the copying stop, but that the author be paid. If the author isn't paid and the technology carries us further, we are going to have to figure out some other ways to pay the author if you want him to write.

Authors are not going to write books for nothing. They don't write for the same reasons college professors do. Authors are not publishing because otherwise they will perish in another profession—teaching. They are writing to make a living, and that's how they make it.

What you come down to, therefore, is a situation where

you would have to provide a substitute for entrepreneurial publishing if you destroy the author's basic copying rights. If an author can't go to a publisher like Random House and have the book published and protected by copyright so the publisher can get his money back and the author can make some income, then someone else will have to do it. That will be either the universities or the state or some other public institutions. Truly copyright, when you come down to it, is the keystone to the existence of private writing and private publishing—in other words, free speech. Once the government gets its hands on it, you would not have Ralph Nader's books published. You would not have books criticizing Mr. Nixon or the Viet Nam war. The government won't do it, and you will end up with the situation *The New York Times* of last Sunday described in its article on Solzhenitsyn, the famous Russian author of *The First Circle* and *Cancer Ward.* "He can still write," says the title of the article, "he just can't publish."

Proprietary Rights and the Distribution of Information

Paul G. Zurkowski

Mr. Zurkowski, who is an attorney, is executive director of the Information Industry Association, Washington, D.C.

There is a feeling that the Information Industry Association is composed of people who arise looking like computers and function during the day like that. I would like to disabuse you of this impression. I would like to suggest as a result that the information industry comes into the problems that have been discussed this morning in a different way. It is such a different way that it is a change in kind as well as a change in degree.

Basically, information industry companies are a wide range of firms which are engaged in the creation and marketing of information products and services through the applications of advanced information and technology. Usually that comes out as the word "computer." Our member companies are to the computer industry what the operating airlines are to the airframe manufacturers. When you say airlines you don't think of Boeing but of the people who are involved in the day-to-day application of the technology—Eastern, American, Trans World.

To reinforce a number of things that were said this morning, it was curious to note that Mr. Lieb and Miss Ringer came out with the same conclusion: There having to be some agreement between the publishers and the librarians. By the separate legislation, Charlie suggested a joint commission. The basic point that needs to be made here is made in part by McLuhan. McLuhan, at one point in *War and Peace in the Global Village,* contends that each new technology tends to create its own service environment which in turn tends to junk the previous service environment.

51

The lectures that you have heard this morning are evidence of that process. In the Gutenberg or ink-print technology, the service environment by which information requirements for people are fulfilled is not through libraries alone, not through publishers alone or not through authors alone but through a structure within which each of these groups plays an integral part. Publishers publish portable files of information—books, journals, etc. Libraries exist to create as complete collections as possible of published materials. Schools, from reading readiness through graduate programs, train people in their use. In fact, the copyright law, whether it is written in 1909 or 1969, is a law that details the rules by which the ink-print service environment functions. As the executive director, I am trying to identify what rules should be applied to the emerging post-Gutenberg or what I have come to call the information service environment.

Each new technology tends to create its own service environment and junk the previous one. I came to see that in terms of a reading problem that my eight-year-old has. He, as a matter of fact, grew up on television. He logged more hours of television prior to reaching first grade than he will log in the classroom by the time he reaches junior high. He has a different way of filing information in his mind other than reading one word after another. He has, and his whole generation has, an image-oriented mentality, and this is a phenomenon of the new information service environment. I submit as an exhibit a publication just out on the market that is titled, *Damn Reading—A Case Against Literacy.* It details all of the arguments in favor of enabling people who handle information differently in their minds to do so and not be required to spend time fighting that system, "learning to read." I don't mean to argue the case for the two educators who wrote this book, but I submit it as evidence that there is concern about the information service environment that is being created which is different from and distinct from libraries.

One area in which the information industry has gotten involved has been proprietary rights. We held a meeting at Airlie House, Virginia, last July, out of which grew a proposal for a change in the national commission.

We have been concerned with what is meant when you

say new technological uses of copyrighted work. I think that I have gotten, from the discussion this morning, an understanding of what the Gutenberg service environment representatives intended by this. But, as an illustration of Miss Ringer's point, these words mean different things to different people. To the information industry, the concept of new technological uses of copyrighted work meant something different than single copying or multiple copying in libraries.

The problem for the commission is, even if enacted today, that it would, at the end of its three-year term, be about where it is today because of the changes that are coming along the road. There are a number of forces developing in this area which are going to create a demand and a system for facilitating the marketing of information through the new technology. I would suggest that this is something that will come to pass in the next three to five years. These are not things that are Utopian; these are very basic developments that are going on now.

The first of these issues, forces or pressures that will arise is a sleeper type—integrity of text. I think that integrity of text is not involved in the discussion this morning and in what you are talking about here, of single-copy copying devices, but it is involved in computerized data basis. When you get a text stored in a computer, all you have in the storage medium is either holes in a card or electric registrations on a magnetic tape, either one of which can be altered rather rapidly and even between computer printouts. So, if you were to construct a world where the information of society was stored on magnetic tapes and you relied strictly on accessing magnetic tapes in order to get the information you need, you would encounter immediately the integrity of text problem. This is because you have no certainty. No judge would accept that printout from the computer as being what it purports to be. He would say, "Give me the best evidence, and this isn't it." He would not take judicial notice of it because he would say, "Just because it is consistent or inconsistent with a previous printout doesn't mean that it is what it purports to be."

In the Gutenberg technology, when you have a press run, the first copy is identical to the last and you can rely on it. If there are pages torn out, you can identify them. But if you have to rely just on computer printouts, whether it would be printed on a large sheet of paper or on microfilm, you would have a problem of certification that this material is what it purports to be. What you would have would be users lining up to you to get certification. In the new technology, there will be requirements on the part of the user for some certainty that what he got is what it purports to be. This is a problem which doesn't exist in the Gutenberg service environment. So there will be a pressure within society for some mechanism by which they can attain the certainty they have come to rely upon in using ink-print materials.

The lack of a system by which people can be certain of this material, the lack of an adequate proprietary rights scheme, will also create a phenomenon in the information area which I call small businessitis. The people who will get into this business are the people who will see an application for the computer technology and who want to spend twenty-four hours a day getting out a product that they can be proud of and on which you can rely. And, as a matter of fact, their reputation is about all that you will be able to rely on until such time as we get a modern proprietary rights scheme. Well, this isn't going to work very well either, because people have been spoon-fed the notion that we are going to have complex networks—that we are going to be able to supply our information needs from one end of the country to the other. The fact is, it depends on getting money to do that, and getting money to do that depends on the ability to make a profit doing that. And making a profit doing that depends on having enough money to invest to have a nationwide system. That isn't going to happen because there isn't any proprietary rights scheme by which enough money can be gotten together to do it properly.

We have two pressures, one coming from the users saying, "Tell us what this is . . . what it claims to be." The other says, "We need to be compensated for each use so we can provide you with the kind of network of nationwide service that, during the next three to five years, will be available only in fairly limited geographic areas."

Part of that pressure for the network concept is going to come from the users segment, because there is a feeling that this technology ought to be able to make these things more efficient and less expensive. There will come a realization even within your own library situation that reliance on the office copier, even as inexpensive as it is per copy and as easy as it is to copy, is still relatively inefficient. This is in comparison to a network concept where you would be able to draw on other collections which you cannot afford to maintain yourselves. It is much like the postal strike situation. Everybody assumes that the mail is cheap and inexpensive because it costs six cents to mail a letter. But when the whole system breaks down and you don't get your mail, you realize that there are inefficiencies. And it doesn't take a complete breakdown; it takes just a delay—a week to get a letter from New York to Washington. It is at this same level of efficiency that, as the library feels more economic pressure on its resources, it is going to feel the need to cooperate and the need to work with other libraries, as well as a need to get into the information service environment and into the information industry type activity.

The fourth pressure that is coming along is a question that Nicholas Johnson of the Federal Communications Commission spoke to, and that is the question of thought control. He is a fairly outspoken advocate of CATV. He challenges the networks from time to time on the grounds that he is concerned that the systems of communications, whether they be cable systems or broadcasting systems, be available and open to any information source. You cannot get a monopoly on the delivery of information systems. But it is my contention that he is worrying about the wrong problem. In order to avoid thought control problems, what is needed in addition to the channels for communicating information is the companion marketing mechanism, the information infrastructure, really, through which the information can move. Take the Smothers Brothers Show, for example. It lost its spot on the network. There were plenty of other television stations across the country that would have loved to have had the program, but no marketing mechanism existed by which the Smothers Brothers program could be marketed on the nationwide level that it needed in order to sustain the economics of producing it.

The final pressure that is coming along relates to the problem of taxes. You will get your tax bill and hear about the problems of pollution—air pollution, water pollution, all sorts of pollution. When society finally gets to putting the money that must be put into those problems in order to be able to sustain life on this planet—and I think that gives these problems some priority—the first victim will be the parochial schools. When the parochial schools go, the domino effect will be that more money will be needed for the public schools. When more money is needed for the public schools, less money will be available for libraries. And the squeeze is already being felt.

Let me report a quote on the other end of the scale. One of the speakers at the meetings that we just held in Washington said that we needed to find new ways to manufacture money. It is my contention that the information industry is in the process of figuring out ways to make money by disseminating information. This amounts to a classic reversal in the value of information. Reuters, the news service, got started and money was made at the time Wellington defeated Napoleon. Reuters had a pigeon that carried the news to London. People who got advance word of that victory made a bundle, and Reuters made a reputation. This is a classic example of building power and wealth through the advance access to private stores of information.

Through the application of the vast advanced information technology, there are people who are just as devoted to serving man's information requirements. A lot of them are aimed at more commercial applications than you care to think about perhaps, but they are devoted to the need to communicate information and they have figured out a way to manufacture money out of disseminating and marketing information.

I relate this observation to the stock market situation. One of these companies is Profile Communications which has computerized news items that have impact on the values of different stocks. Ben Weil has some stock. He would get one profile list of news on a weekly basis that effects the values of the stock he has in his portfolio, and I would get a separate file of information on the stock that I am interested in following. Profile Communications would make money out of it because they are selling information, and Ben Weil and I would make money out of it because we would be able to anticipate changes in the stock market.

Let me close with one final example of the reversal of information. In the Congress there is an office called Parliamentarian. At first glance it does not appear to be a very important office. However, when you realize that the precedents of the Speaker of the House have been published through 1937 and that every other decision of the Speaker that has taken place since then is maintained in a newspaper size looseleaf file in the Parliamentarian's office, you see the value of a private store of information. In order for a Congressman to debate a parliamentary point on the floor of the House, he has to go to the Parliamentarian the day before and say, "How would you rule?" The Parliamentarian, since he has the only source, is able to say, "Well, I'd cite this 1942 decision of the Speaker." And where is the Congressman? He has no choice but to go along with the decision. As a result, the Parliamentarian has a place of power and a source of wealth.

What I am trying to relate here for you bears only a vague resemblance to this question of photocopying in libraries. The problem of copying is a problem of the Gutenberg service environment. The resolution of this problem alone will not be sufficient to enable you to continue to perform the valuable functions you perform in the new emerging service environment. There are many other forces that are impacting on that new environment, a few of which I have referred to. I suggest that you have to pay attention to them as well.

Libraries—On the Spot with Present and Future Copyright Legislation

Verner W. Clapp

Mr. Clapp is consultant to the Council on Library Resources, Washington, D.C., of which he was president from its beginning in 1956 until his retirement in 1967. Prior to that he was with the Library of Congress for 35 years in various capacities.

Until recently, librarians and the copyright industry—authors, publishers, etc.—collaborated very happily. I remind you that after copyright had banged around in a number of government agencies—the district courts, the State Department, the Patent Office, and even, to an extent, the Smithsonian Institution—it was finally welcomed into the Library of Congress. There in 1870 the Librarian of Congress was required "to perform all acts and duties required by law touching copyright." It has been there ever since, and there has never been a serious move to take it out.

The Copyright Act of 1909, under which we currently live, as well as the present Copyright Revision Bill (S.543), were both initially drafted in the Copyright Office in the Library of Congress. The first form of the act of 1909 was presented to the Committees on Patents of the House of Representatives and of the Senate, which were responsible for copyright in those days, at a joint meeting in the Senate Reading Room in the Library of Congress. It was quite a notable occasion; Mark Twain was there in his white linen suit, and the big wigs of the copyright industry—authors, publishers, lawyers—were well represented. The bill was elegantly introduced by Herbert Putnam, the Librarian of Congress, himself a lawyer, a member of the New York Bar and a member of a well-known publishing family which had besides a particular interest in copyright.

The library and publishing worlds may in consequence regard the past as providing very good precedent for the kind of collaboration that Mr. Lieb has suggested to us. I told him during the intermission that I have made just such a suggestion for collaboration to a principal representative of the copyright interests of the publishers, and I regret that it has not been taken up. I hope that the suggestion may now bear fruit.

I speak of a happy collaboration. Nevertheless, there have been from time to time clouds on the horizon, perhaps no larger than a man's hand, and they have impaired the happy relationship on several occasions. While the 1909 act was in transit through the houses of Congress, the question of importation by libraries of copies of foreign editions of books copyrighted in the United States came up. The publishers wished to prevent such importation. The libraries objected vehemently; they wished to be free to import such books when needed, as, for example, when the foreign edition might contain a preface or some other material not available in the domestic edition, and there broke out a short-lived feud between the publishers and the librarians. But when the publishers really understood the issue, the matter was settled amicably in the librarians' favor.

However, the same issue has arisen several times since in connection with attempts to revise the copyright law. And so strong were feelings that at one time, Dr. M. L. Raney, the librarian of the University of Chicago, was not on speaking terms with such a mild man as Frederick Melcher of the R. R. Bowker Company. When two people like that are not on speaking terms, then something is really bad. As a matter of fact, the importation issue isn't completely dead now; its traces can be found in S.543, where importation rights are no longer given to libraries as such, but only as governmental, scholarly, educational or religious organizations.

When these clouds grow larger than a man's hand, they are a warning to librarians, consumers and others as well that publishers are not in business for their health.

The publishers are owners of a monopoly, *pace* Mr. Clark. Chief Justice Hughes called it a monopoly [in Fox Film Co. vs. Doyal, 286 *US* 123, 127 (1932)], and I shall not dissent. So long as librarians conceived of copyright as a commendable system for preventing piracy and plagiarism and for assuring authors and publishers of the just fruit of their labors, it never occurred to them (the librarians) that they themselves would ever be found guilty of infringement. They could therefore collaborate with completely clear consciences and no selfconsciousness. But publishers, they discovered from time to time with some surprise, were monopolists. Now, from the point of view of the owner of a monopoly, it is a device to enable you to make money. And, of course, you *should* make money, especially if you are the officer of a corporate body responsible to stockholders. You should neglect no opportunity to profit from your monopoly, especially since it is, by law, of limited duration. From time to time this duty of copyright proprietors to make a profit on their monopoly comes up, and it has done so in rather exaggerated form in connection with S.543.

In 1968, the latest year for which I have data, American libraries disposed of something like $350 million in book funds. This, to coin a phrase, isn't peanuts. Almost all of this money is destined for the coffers of the copyright industry. This, however, doesn't seem to be enough, and the industry wishes to take advantage of its monopoly to make even more.

From the point of view of Congress, which gets its directive in this matter from the Constitution, the copyright monopoly is not merely for the purpose of making money. Its primary purpose, by contrast, is to serve the public interest. Let me quote from the Constitution: "The Congress shall have power to promote the progress of science and useful arts [I emphasize these words] by securing for limited times to authors and inventors exclusive rights to their respective writings and discoveries." Every copyright act written under the authority of this Constitutional provision represents an attempt to reconcile a conflict between public and private interest.

This conflict goes back a long way in time. American copyright history starts in Great Britain and goes back at least to 1478. In that year, the first year of the reign of King Richard III, an act of Parliament encouraged the importation of printed publications into the kingdom. There was as yet practically no domestic printing industry in England at that time, printing being a very recently invented device and England one of the last European countries to receive its benefits.

By 1533, however, the domestic printing industry had flourished to the point where it desired protection from foreign competition. In that year, the twenty-fifth of Henry VIII, an act of Parliament gave it the protection it sought. But then Parliament, fearful lest the domestic industry should take undue advantage of protection, set up a mechanism to control book prices. A complainant might submit his plea to an extensive and notable list of officials, even to the king himself; and the official would be obligated to set matters straight. This procedure was, of course, never really effective; printing and publishing formed a much too complicated and socially-involved business for such simple control.

During the sixteenth and seventeenth centuries, there came into the hands of the publishers, for one reason or another, an effective monopoly on publication, and one that was to all intents and purposes permanent. From time to time the public became very exacerbated by the abuses to which this permanent monopoly led, giving rise to a demand for enforcement of the price control provisions of the act of 1533. In 1694 a committee of Parliament studying the situation submitted a list of complaints of the publishing system as it was operating at that time. The first copyright act, the Statute of Ann, 1709, was primarily an act to control these abuses arising from the publishers' permanent monopoly. It was a tough act. It terminated the permanent monopoly, substituting one which was limited initially to fourteen years, renewable for an equal period. It made it possible for authors to share the copyright. It reinstated in even more elaborate form the price control provisions of Henry VIII.

Thereupon there ensued, as Professor Ray Lyman Patterson of the Vanderbilt University Law School has told us (in his *Copyright in Historical Perspective*, 1968), a relentless battle on the part of the publishers to regain the lost permanent monopoly, using authors as their stalking horse. This battle has continued right down to the present day and is one in which the copyright industry has been pretty successful. It very soon succeeded in quashing the price control provisions of the Statute of Ann. It has succeeded in doubling the period both of the original and the renewal term, and a series of enactments in the past few years has extended this renewal term in the prospect that the entire term will be set at the life of the author plus fifty years. In addition, copyright, which consisted originally merely in the monopoly of printing the copyrighted work, has since been extended to include rights of public performance, translation, condensation and adaptation.

As the rights of copyright proprietors have gained, those of purchasers of copies of copyrighted works have diminished. In 1709 the purchaser of a copy of a copyrighted work—specifically, a book—had the right to read it silently or aloud, in private or in public, whether or not for profit. He could translate it, abridge it or dramatize it. If it was a dramatic work, he could perform it publicly or privately, whether or not for profit. He could copy from it for purposes of study or research. He could exhibit it or lend it whether for profit or not, sell it, give it away or destroy it, use it for a door-stop or a missile. The only thing that he clearly might not do was to reprint or otherwise bootleg it.

Today this purchaser has lost a number of those rights. Specifically, he may not perform a literary work publicly for profit. For example, he may not read it aloud for profit if it is a story or a poem, nor deliver it for profit if it is a lecture, sermon or address. He may not translate it, abridge it or adapt it. If it is a dramatic work, he may not perform it publicly even if this is not for profit, and this prohibition runs to dramatic motion pictures and literary and musical compositions as well as to plays per se. He may still exhibit, lend, sell, give away, throw it at his wife or burn it. Although he may still copy from it for purposes of study, or permit another to do so, his rights in this connection are badly clouded by the language of the Copyright Act of 1909—a cloud which has not been removed or clarified by litigation.

The extension of the copyright in the area of performance has given rise to a noteworthy development, the application of the not-for-profit principle. This principle has furnished, in a very striking manner, the basis for mediation between the private and the public interests in copyright. The development emerged in the Copyright Act of 1909. That act was infused with a tender regard for the public interest. As a matter of fact, a number of passages in the reports which accompanied the act in its transit through Congress are classic statements of the status of the public interest in copyright legislation, and if I had time I would read them to you. (See especially *House Report 2222*, 60th Congress, pages 6–7.) The not-for-profit provision reflected this regard for the public interest. It arose in this way.

Performance rights had been invented for dramatic works in 1856 and had been extended to music in 1894. In 1909 they were again extended to sermons, lectures, and addresses, but this extension, as well as the one to music, was at that time tempered by limiting the rights to for-profit performance, leaving non-profit performance exempt. And in 1952, when performance rights were still further extended to non-dramatic literary and musical works and recordings thereof, the not-for-profit principle was reiterated by Congress with emphasis.

Now, however, comes S.543, the Ninety-First Congress version of the copyright revision bill, a direct descendant of H. R. 2512 of the Ninetieth Congress which was actually passed by the lower house on April 11, 1967. H. R. 2512 was explicitly an industry bill. Its purpose (as stated in *House Report 83*, 90th Congress, page 3) was to insure the profits of the copyright proprietor, while the public interest, in contrast to the corresponding report in 1909, was not mentioned. The Copyright Office, which—as in 1909—had drafted the initial bill, has similarly subordinated the public to the private interest in its report recommending the legislation (*Copyright Law Revision*, Part 6, 1965, page 14). As for the not-for-profit principle, the Copyright Office, after accepting it in 1961 as the mediating principle between monopoly and the public interest, abandoned it completely in 1965 on the grounds that a non-profit use might displace a profitable one (*Ibid.*, pages 14, 21). To this the Congressional committee added that some non-profit users are quite able to pay royalties (*House Report 83*, page 26). In these views the public interest in copyright appears to be limited to an interest in having an opportunity to pay royalties for the use of copyrighted material.

The legislative results of this anxiety of the Copyright Office and of the Congressional committee to make it possible for the copyright proprietor to neglect no opportunity for profiting from his monopoly, accompanied by a very restricted view of the nature of the public interest in copyright, may be guessed. In the first place, instead of stating the rights of copyright proprietors in specific and narrow terms, as has been the approach of all previous copyright enactments, S.543 expresses them in global and encompassing terms, and when exceptions must be made to these globally-expressed rights, they are made minimally and grudgingly.

For example, where in the 1909 act the distribution right was limited to selling, previously defined by the Supreme Court as being limited to the first sale, in S.543 it is extended to distribution generally, whether by sale or other transfer of ownership, or by rental, lease or lending. At a later point, purchasers of copies of copyrighted works are given a "privilege" of selling or otherwise disposing of them as a specific limitation upon the overall right of the proprietors. It may be noted that rental, lease and lending are not mentioned in this limitation.

Similarly, S.543 gives the proprietor overall rights of display. At a later point, purchasers of copies are given a certain "privilege" of display, again as a limitation upon the global rights of the proprietor.

It may be readily admitted that for libraries the principal effects of the provisions just cited are not very great. If S.543 were enacted, libraries would presumably still be able to rent, sell, lend and dispose of their books. They will still be able to display their wares in their lobbies, although they will no longer be able to show them on television. But genuine injury is done by these provisions, though at the moment it appears academic. Specifically, this bandit-like grabbing of the purchaser's clear title of ownership and substituting for it an inferior and revocable "privilege" opens the way to serious encroachment on the rights of libraries, for example, through the creation of the so-called "public lending right". This is a device by which, in Denmark and Sweden, public libraries are required to pay royalties upon their circulation into a fund which is disbursed to the domestic authors of these countries. There the tax is justified by the small populations and little-used languages. However, in Great Britain the "right" is being actively promoted, without these justifications, by the Arts Council and the Authors' League. In the United States, little has as yet been heard of it, but serious consideration was given to incorporating it into the current copyright revision bill, and it was apparently excluded only because of the practical difficulties of implementing it (*Copyright Law Revision*, Part 6, page 31). It is obvious that at any time that these practical difficulties do not seem to be insuperable, the "right" can be claimed as actually already in existence under the overall exclusive title in their works claimed for the copyright proprietors in S.543. I expect to see the day when all use will be subject to royalty; we will pay royalty whenever we use an IBM computer or a Xerox copier, or read a book or sit on a chair. The opportunity to impose a permanent tax is irresistible.

Of greater immediate practical importance, though not only to libraries, is the proposed extension of the copyright term to life-of-the-author-plus-fifty-years. This is an approximate doubling of the present twenty-eight-plus-twenty-eight years. It constitutes quite a stride toward the recovery of the publishers' lost permanent copyright. It is justified on the ground that it is the term employed by the Berne Copyright Union and is regarded as the "foundation of the entire bill" (*House Report 83*, page 100). My objection is that in the whole extended discussion of revision, now approximately a decade, the cost of this proposed extension of term has never been studied. This cost, which will have to be borne by the American public, may or may not be large; whatever it is, it is being requested as a gift by the copyright industry.

Meanwhile, at the very moment in which it is asking the taxpayers to double the term and to extend the content of its monopoly, the copyright industry has suddenly become very feisty about what it chooses to call freeloading by libraries in the photocopying of copyrighted materials. This the industry wishes to prohibit as a free practice, even though (a) it is a not-for-profit activity; even though (b) it is known to be essential to the efficient conduct of study and research and thus in the interest of authorship which should be supposed to be of some concern to the industry; even though (c) it is a practice of long standing that goes back to before the Act of 1909 which seems (but only seems) to prohibit it and that was expressly sanctioned thirty-five years ago by the trade association of publishers; even though (d) all studies that have been made of it indicate that it does not cause loss of sales to publishers but may indeed lead to additional sales; even though (e) it is well known that the cost of collecting royalties on the practice would be so high as to erase any profit; even though (f) the practice would seem to come within the doctrine of "fair use" which has been unctuously (because meaninglessly) written into S.543; and, finally, even though (g) those against whom the prohibition is chiefly hurled, and the only ones against whom it could be executed, are the publishers' best customers, namely, libraries.

The library groups had assumed that single-copy photocopying was legalized by the doctrine of fair use, and they had requested of the Congressional committee only that this doctrine be acknowledged by the new act. They were, in consequence, thunderstruck when the bill (H.R.4347, Eighty-Ninth Congress) was reported out on October 12, 1966, with an acknowledgment of fair use, to be sure, but with an interpretation of it that appeared to disqualify library single-copying.

Specifically, although H.R. 4347 acknowledged fair use as a limitation upon the exclusive rights of copyright proprietors and listed the criteria for determining fair use, the doctrine did not emerge as the protectress of library photocopying in the report (*House Report 2237*, Eighty-Ninth Congress) accompanying the bill. The committee explained that it did not favor a specific provision dealing with library photocopying, nor even special fair use provisions regarding such copying. This left library photocopying subject to the regular doctrine of fair use—in other words, in order to find out whether its practice is legal, a library must submit to trial so that the practice can be tested by a court, for fair use is court-administered doctrine. And while the committee emphasized that it had no intention of enlarging or narrowing the doctrine of fair use in any way, yet it permitted itself to say that where unauthorized copying displaces what realistically might have been a sale, no matter how minor the amount of money involved, the interests of the owner need protection.

This last would appear to nullify fair use as a justification of library photocopying.

The report concluded by urging all concerned to resume their efforts to reach an accommodation under which the needs of scholarship and the rights of authors would both be respected. A courageous stand for a legislative committee!

H.R.4347 was introduced into the Ninetieth Congress as

H.R.2512, the report was reissued in substantially its original form as *House Report 83*, and the bill was passed by the House of Representatives, as I have said, on April 11, 1967. S.543 of the Ninety-First Congress is its lineal descendant.

The Senate has expanded Section 108 of the bill so as to respond to the clamor from the library world following the passage of H.R.2512. This expanded section comes close to meeting library needs (But—alas!—a miss is as good as a mile!). It extends to libraries the authorization to make copies for security purposes that was limited in H.R.2512 to archives; it authorizes replacement copying and it authorizes copying for service to readers, either directly or through another institution. The last, of course, is the crux of the matter. There are, of course, a few little conditions. These are:

a. No more than one copy may be made ("One copy" is later carefully defined.).
b. The copying shall not be for the purpose of direct or indirect commercial advantage.
c. The collections of the copying library must be open to the public or available to researchers in the field.
d. The material copied shall not be a musical, pictorial, graphic or sculptural work, or a motion picture or other audio-visual work.
e. The user must establish to the satisfaction of the library that an unused copy cannot be obtained at a normal price from commonly-known trade sources in the United States, including authorized reproducing services.
f. The copy must become the property of the user.
g. The library must have no notice that the copy would be used for other purposes than private study, scholarship or research.
h. The library must display prominently at the place where orders are accepted and include on its order form a warning of copyright in wording prescribed by the Register of Copyrights. (But the bill also exempts the use of unsupervised photocopying machines that display a warning regarding copyright.)

All but two of these conditions are quite acceptable to libraries. Of these, condition d. is crippling but not fatal. But condition e. is fatal. It would send the users of libraries back to the Middle Ages, compelled to copy out by manual drudgery materials needed for their research (and there is no showing that this is any more legal than photocopying). It would kill the vast exchange of interlibrary loans of journal articles which is possible only because libraries can send photocopies in lieu of the bound volumes which they are unwilling to lend on account of cost, risk of damage or loss and deprivation of their use.

My friends on the panel would have it that libraries do not need specific authorization to photocopy for interlibrary loan, that this would be justified as fair use. The fact is, of course, that no one knows what is fair use in library photocopying because there has never been a court case on the matter. And if it were indeed clear that library photocopying were justified by fair use, what was the purpose of all the very expert drafting that went into Section 108? So long as the condition that I have labeled e. persists in the bill, librarians will have no choice but to oppose the legislation. It seems to me, in consequence, that it is in the long-term interest of publishers to collaborate with librarians toward an early settlement of this matter.

PART III

Panel Discussion

ROY L. KIDMAN, MODERATOR: As I came in this morning, some people asked me how I was going to get the panel to start talking. I guess I don't have to worry about that anymore. I would just like to make one observation, since I am a librarian, that the librarians are ending up just like they usually do, that is, in the middle of the whole thing, trying to protect the authors on one side and the users on the other. Perhaps all of the opinions of other people are summed up by Mr. Karp's plaintive remarks that "we are not asking the librarians to pay." We know that, but we are concerned about our users.

I am going to ask a question of Mr. Lieb by making this observation. The economics of this situation are perhaps not the overriding factor from the librarian's point of view. Rather, it is the time involved. If we have a patron before us, we might be willing to get another copy or a reprint or whatever. But here is this person before us whom we would like to serve well, but the mechanisms which you described are mechanisms which don't provide for that kind of response. I wonder if you've thought about that at all.

MR. LIEB: Yes, I have thought about it. The answer is difficult. There are two questions. I think that as we get away from the partisan points of view, the problem is quite clear. I don't think that anybody really believes, contrary to Mr. Clapp's oratory, that librarians have a right to copy fully and to give without limitations. This has the potential to remove the market for published works, and, when that happens, it's no good for anybody.

The problem is as Mr. Kidman stated. Publishers—and I say this sincerely—don't say you can't photocopy. Up to now they've said, don't photocopy because nobody's thought of a way to balance the thing so the publisher and the author will come out where they should come out. This is the problem.

First, I accept that the librarian must photocopy; I said this in my paper. Secondly, it means that there can't be a long wait until the librarian writes to the publisher and gets an answer weeks later. I accept that, too. The challenge before librarians, authors, publishers and really the entire book community—the community dealing in intellectual works—is how to handle photocopy requests. It is conceivable that in certain kinds of publishing, the problem may not be as difficult as it seems to be. I have a theory that if you break things down into segments of publishing, we may find answers which will satisfy some if not all of the segments.

If you start with journal publishing, the solution may be in the subscription price. If the publisher offers his journal at subscription price A for single copy reading and he offers the same magazine or journal at subscription price B, which would be price A plus a reasonable surcharge for the right to make photocopies, you would perhaps pay subscription price B because you will know that you will be called upon for photocopies. Also notwithstanding Mr. Clapp's fears, there is not likely to be profiteering, because journal publishing is as competitive as almost everything else. The laws of economics would make the price realistic.

Journal publishing, therefore, would not require a complex mechanism. The problem is more difficult when you get to the copying of articles, chapters and books. And this is where I think a committee should set to work to first find the facts. The way I would do it is to give out a dozen scholarships and place the recipients to work in the library. We would have, for the purpose of research for the joint use of library, publisher, author, government and anybody else who is interested, a day-by-day account of what goes on in a photocopy room. And in a year or so, we would be able to trim the problem down so that we could, at least for a time, eliminate most of the abuses.

MR. ZURKOWSKI: I'd like to address myself to one of the implications in your statement that the librarian is essentially part of the service elite who is conceiving of ways in which information requirements are to be fulfilled. I would suggest that more and more in the future the librarian at the front desk will have to concede that what happens at that desk is a business transaction in the form of delivery of information. What happens behind that front desk and in the back room where the catalogs are maintained and, in fact, where the complete administration of the library is, all becomes justifiable in terms of the information delivered not in terms of how wide the collection is or whether it is complete. You are going to be able to call on other sources of information, and acquiring this information is going to cost more money. And this money will come from other sources than your current sources for building a collection. Furthermore, when what you are asked for is contained and produced out of a tape, you are into a different ball game and into a business situation that requires you to think in terms of business transactions and not simply in anticipating and fulfilling a community desire for a particular piece of published work.

MR. CLAPP: I wish to continue along the lines of Mr. Lieb, and I don't want to disturb Mr. Lieb. Concerning your suggestion for discussions, I would be very happy to be involved in an attempt to get them going. As I said this morning, I actually made the same kind of suggestion myself, and I often wonder why it was not accepted. I still don't know why it wasn't accepted. You should know, however, that I'll support the recommendation of House Bill 2512 of the last session. They urged the parties to get together. And the parties did get together under the auspices of the Copyright Office, but, as Miss Ringer said this morning, those conversations weren't fruitful. If anything, they were retrograde. I'm not going to venture an opinion why they were retrograde, because this might be regarded as partisan, but the fact is that such conversations have not been altogether neglected. But now Mr. Lieb says that one of the first things this group should do is to find out exactly what happens. I'm not at all averse to that. Let me remark, Mr. Lieb, that there have been four studies of what happens to photocopying in the library. There was the study undertaken by the Joint Libraries Committee on Fair Use in Photocopying—actually not undertaken by the committee itself but on its behalf by attorneys of some distinction in the city of New York. There was another study undertaken by a Cleveland firm on behalf of the National Science Foundation. The third study, although not directed to the point of view of the use of photocopy, was by the American Book Publishers Council itself. And a fourth study was by a group known as the Committee to Investigate Copyright Problems, under a contract from the U.S. Office of Education. None of these found that the proprietors are greatly damaged by photocopy, if at all. Indeed, one of them, the National Science Foundation study, actually suggested that subscriptions to periodicals were promoted by photocopy. This is the result of institutions acting on the recommendation of persons finding through a photocopy what the value of a particular journal is. In any case, if the publishers were willing to accept the results of these studies, we'd have the question you raised answered.

I gather from this morning's discussion that we have a misunderstanding as to the intention of Sections 107 and 108 of the pending bill. I gather from what other speakers have said that they regard Section 107—the "fair use" section or the section that states the criteria for fair use—as covering that kind of photocopying which libraries now do a few pages at a time. And Section 108 is intended, by contrast, to extend to those cases which the drafters believe librarians wish to go, namely, to copying of entire works. Now I am speculating that this may be the interpretation of these other speakers, but I don't know. In any case, libraries do not read the bill this way.

Libraries read the bill to state that in 107 there are certain criteria by which fair use is adjudged, and the activities of libraries will be adjudged by these criteria when they are adjudicated in the courts. So all this Section 107 does for libraries is to threaten to haul them into court for what they consider to be perfectly normal activities. Librarians also read Section 108 as referring to copies of entire works. Copying entire works is not normal library practice. We just don't normally copy entire works; it's inefficient. Why should a library copy an entire work if the work can be secured any other way? It's ridiculous. I gather from the morning's discussions that Section 108 is nevertheless intended to supply us with authority to do entire-work copying under certain conditions. We have attempted to show the drafters of the bill that Section 107 is no good for us unless it is accompanied by something which tells us what fair use is. Others were talking this morning about fair use copying as if it was all we wanted. But nobody knows what it is. There isn't a single case to describe what fair use copying is.

MR. ZURKOWSKI: I have one of the tables from one of the reports—the C.I.C.P. report. It documents a level of copying which I think would be considered to be to the advantage of the publishers. This is from the Office of Education, Project 70793 by the Committee to Investigate Copyright Problems. Included in the survey during the month of March, 1967, were the following libraries: Fort Detrick, Bowdoin, Harvard, John Crearer, Lockheed and Stanford Law. Listed in the C.I.C.P. report are the works and numbers of publishers copied —Bowdoin, 60; Fort Detrick, 93; Harvard, 158; John Crearer, 482; Lockheed, 142, and Stanford Law, 25. The total number of pages of books copied that month by these libraries was 9,126, and the total pages of journals copied by these libraries was 31,000. The total materials in page numbers copied by these libraries was 43,000 in one month. I dare say that this sustains the proposition that copying is a publishing enterprise.

MR. CLAPP: Let me read for you a passage from a pamphlet entitled, "Copyright, a Librarian's View", by my favorite author. It was prepared for the National Advisory Commission of Libraries and is published in the book called *Libraries at Large* (Bowker). It is also separately published by the Copyright Committee of the Association of Research Libraries and is available, free, on request. This discusses the C.I.C.P. report:

"In 1967 the Committee to Investigate Copyright Problems conducted under contract to the U.S. Office of Education a study of photocopying in libraries. It concluded among other things that: 97% of library photocopying consists of single copies; 90% of the materials copied in U.S. libraries are less than ten years old; 54–59% of the material copied is copyrighted; over a billion copyrighted pages were copied in the U.S. in 1967.

"The Committee did not particularly study the question of damage to publishers resulting from photocopying, but contrasts the cumulative effect of much copying with the not-measurable damage of a single copy."

In other words, it said, we have not gone into the question

of the damage done to the proprietors through all this copying because it was not ascertainable. But it must be obvious to everybody, it said, that where so much copying was done, there must be some damage. This is substantial, Mr. Zurkowski said.

I deny that this is the case at all. The mere fact of multiplication doesn't add up to damage in any particular case. As I said this morning, the facts of the situation belied Mr. Zurkowski's conclusion. The first Xerox machine was introduced into the White House in March, 1960. So we have had just a little over ten years of the improved photocopying devices. In that time, sales of periodicals and books have gone up like crazy just at the time when, according to the claims that are made, publishers should be going into bankruptcy and authors should be starving in separate attic cells.

MR. KARP: Mr. Clapp has a way with figures. He told you people that this bill was produced by the industry. This is utter nonsense. It was the Copyright Office by the request of the Congress which prepared this bill. To put it bluntly, as far as authors are concerned, we would be perfectly happy with the present provisions of the present law as they relate to copying. We haven't asked for any changes in copying; they have—your representatives have.

Mr. Clapp, for some reason or another, I think has probably made a psychological faux pas on the term of copyright. He says, look at these greedy people. They want to double the present term of copyright. The present term is fifty-six years. Double the present term is 112 years. John O'Hara died this week. He had a book that hadn't been published yet. On the basis of life plus fifty years, the life of that book's copyright, no matter when it is published, would be fifty years from his death. If it is published tomorrow under the life and fifty years, the total term of copyright on that book would already be six years shorter than it is under the present law. Now, that isn't 112 years; that is fifty years. And that's not longer, that's shorter than the present term.

Actually, the Copyright Office did a study of the average term of copyright based on life and fifty years, which varies depending on how long the author lives. For the man who writes a few books and dies young, fifty years would be very short. The fact of the matter is that for most American authors, books produced late in their careers would have less copyright protection under the system we asked for than they have right now. On the average, the study concluded, the new bill would add nineteen years. Nineteen years added to fifty-six is seventy-five years. Seventy-five, according to my arithmetic is not double fifty-six which Mr. Clapp suggested. It falls far short of 112, which is his figure.

Authors aren't the primary "spokesmen" of the bill. One reason we want life and fifty is that it is a much simpler system of copyright and it is the system we must have if we are going to enter the Berne International Copyright Convention. Every other country in the world that belongs to that convention has life plus fifty years or more. The reason that they do is because these other countries recognize that for a reasonable period of time an author and then his family are entitled to some benefit from the works he has written and created. Life and fifty years is a simple, easily-measurable way of doing it.

The next time you want to buy a New American Library copy of a play by Shakespeare, tell the bookseller that you don't want to pay that seventy-five cents. That is the same price they are asking for a Tennessee Williams play, and Shakespeare is in the public domain, so why aren't you getting it for less. Next time you go to the Metropolitan Opera and they are performing not Copland or Barber or whomever of the few American composers they do, but instead the opera is in the public domain, you try to get the tickets any cheaper.

The copyright committees of both houses of Congress rejected the idea that the life plus fifty term of copyright causes any loss to the public. It simply doesn't. The fact of the matter is that it is mechanically more administrable. It is what the rest of the world employs, because the rest of the world found it fair. And for those few authors who create works of lasting value, it gives them assurance of copyright payment.

Those of you interested in access by the public and by the scholar should know that it ends perpetual common law copyright. I can cite you example after example of works, by Mark Twain and by many other American authors, written in the eighteenth and nineteenth centuries, which will not even go into copyright for another twenty or thirty years, when the people who hold the manuscripts decide to publish them. At that point, the works will then be copyrighted under Mr. Clapp's favorite system and thus will have as much as 300 years of copyright protection. This is as opposed to the proposed system of life and fifty years under which they already would have been in the public domain.

Now let's get back to the original question. According to the study which Mr. Clapp quoted to you, two billion pages, not one billion, were copied in 1967, of which one billion were copyrighted material. And the Copyright Office report says, "Photocopying is increasing on all fronts, and the prospect is for continued increase in the future. The incentive for photocopy is constantly growing as accessible and convenient equipment increases and as the cost of photocopy decreases. The vast majority of photocopying from published works with copyright protection is done without seeking the permission of the Copyright Office and without payment." The threat is there, but it is almost unimportant to start studying the dimensions of the threat. Those of us who have seen the advantages of the Xerox machine and those of us who have seen copying done in universities because it is cheaper than buying books, realize that the threat will increase.

What we are talking about now is a copyright law which would have been adopted had both houses of Congress passed the revision bill. Once revised, it probably would have stayed in effect for another sixty years. As anybody who has followed the copyright history of the past sixty years knows, it is impossible to change the law of copyright in one step, fast. In 1909, there was a little box called the jukebox. It was a device for playing phonograph records that was placed in the penny arcade. And it was played for the owner's profit. The Congress voted into law an exemption which allowed the businessmen who put the machines in these penny arcades to perform the composer's music by playing records, without paying them. Congress gave a special privilege. The argument was that the jukebox was only a toy; it was too expensive and who in the world would put money in the box to hear a record. Today the jukebox industry grosses several hundred million, or probably over a billion, dollars a year from just playing composers' music, and they still don't pay a cent to the composer.

We have here a jukebox—that's what these copying machines are. They are dispensing printed pages. Within limits, there would be no copying fee—on copying within the limit of fair use. Of course, when we go beyond that limit, we are going to hurt someone. We are creating a new medium in which people are paying their money to have copies of copyrighted works. What are we doing about this? Nobody is saying stop. Nobody is saying that you should pick up the phone and call Random House every time you want a copy of part of a book of poetry they have put out.

I'm going to digress a minute. I don't want to be pictured as a defender of publishers because I have enough grievances against them; grievances probably more serious than Mr. Clapp's, because I oppose them on many points. But it is an insult to people like Alfred Knopf or the people at Random House to say they are nothing but profiteering bandits who run around trying to squeeze the last dollar out of a copyright. I would like to have a dollar for every dollar that Mr. Knopf has lost over his publishing career publishing books of verse or of literary criticism or books on some special issues where he knew the day he put out the book he wouldn't get his investment back. But as a publisher with the public interest at heart, he was willing to put his money into the cost of that book and of distribution, knowing that he would not recover. If I had a dollar for every dollar he lost this way, I'd be a millionaire and I wouldn't be spending my time worrying about the poor American author, at least not worrying about him for a living.

Getting back to our solution to the copying problems, what obviously has to be done as time goes on is to work out a system for immediate automatic clearance and for payment of a fee. Mr. Lieb suggested one system which would work for magazines. In fact, Williams and Wilkins offered such a system to the National Medical Library under which an additional charge was made for a magazine when a library wanted some subscription copies. It is not so shocking that a library should be asked to do this considering that they distribute the copies free. In other words, the government is using your money and mine to pay for the copies which they distribute. What Williams and Wilkins are saying is that you are paying all that money to the Xerox company and to the paper manufacturer. All that is being asked for is a small additional fee to cover the loss to the publisher.

There are other ways that have been suggested. One, for example, would be a per-charge fee which the user would pay when he paid the New York Public Library so much for a photocopy. The library would just tack on another five, ten or fifteen cents, depending on the number of pages copied. At the end of the month or at the end of the quarter, the library would transmit those fees to a central clearing house which would then distribute them.

I have been asked by one or two of you how the libraries would do this. Well, for the last fifty years, American composers have made most of their income by just such a system. Every time a song is played on radio or television in this country, a fee is paid which ultimately goes to the composer. A nickle or a dime is not sent to him by mail. The radio or television station pays an annual license fee to a licensing society such as ASCAP. ASCAP collects all license fees and has the responsibility of distributing that money, which has been rather substantial in recent years, among the 30,000 or 40,000 composers who are listed in the ASCAP catalog. The way ASCAP does it is to sample the uses over the year of each member's compositions. Then, by projecting by formulas, it decides how much money each song has earned.

That is one way of handling this. There are about six different ways, and no one is sitting here prescribing *the* method. The ASCAP method has been suggested and the C.I.C.P. committee has suggested another. Probably the ultimate solution would lie with the presidential commission which would be created under Senator McClellan's bill if this proposal passes. Even if it isn't passed, there still would have to be some study by a qualified commission to look into the whole problem of both computer uses and reprography and come up with a licensing system.

MR. LIEB: We seem to have some agreement on the platform that publishers and librarians need to talk to each other on this topic, but I would like to add a corollary note to the suggestion. That is that if and when librarians and publishers begin to talk about this problem again, they might appoint completely new spokesmen. I suggest this because I think there are on both sides, one, two, three or four identifiable men who have been talking about this subject, mostly to themselves, for the last fifteen years. They have become so polarized that they really find it quite difficult to dig themselves out of entrenched positions. I don't believe that the whole library profession or the whole publishing industry is quite as entangled as these small groups are.

Mr. Clapp is bothered by the cloudiness of the fair use concept. I am bothered by the cloudiness of some of his concepts. For example, he tells us that it is not in the librarians' minds to copy whole works. But what does Mr. Clapp mean by "whole work?" An article is a complete entity, a whole work. You cannot tell me, Mr. Clapp, that it is not in a librarian's mind to copy these; they do it by the thousands every day.

Then there is another kind of copying—single copying. We all know that books are bought in single copies originally, as Mr. Karp said earlier today. They are also copied in single copies, mostly in libraries. But how many single copies make multiple copying? When a professor prescribes that an article be read by forty students in his class, and forty students come in individually and ask for a single copy, are you or are you not publishing forty single copies? Cloudy, Mr. Clapp, just as cloudy as fair use.

MR. CLAPP: I hesitate to get into a definition exercise. Before we start a program like this one here today, perhaps we should lay down a whole series of definitions as the copyright bill does. It doesn't use this phrase "whole works." When I use the phrase "whole works," I am referring to an admittedly ambiguous entity since I haven't defined it but which I believe is implied by the language of Section 108. You see, the contrast is between Section 107, which lists the criteria by which fair use is to be adjudged. Then comes Section 108. It appears to me presumptive that the permissions given under Section 108 are to be measured by the fair use provisions of 107. But I judge from what was said this morning that others do not consider that this is the case. Instead,

I judge that they consider that Section 107 is intended to cover one kind of photocopying (the kind of photocopying which would be limited to an article or to an editorial or to a page or two), while Section 108 is intended by contrast to refer to the copying of the entire issue of the *Atlantic Monthly* for March, 1970, or to an entire book—i.e., a whole work. Now I am speculating as a result of this morning's discussion. I do not know if this was in fact in the minds of those who drafted the bill. It sounds like it from what Mr. Lieb was, as well as what other speakers, maybe what Mr. Karp, were saying. These are two different things, and the libraries have not been able to see them.

MISS RINGER: I think the audience has seen a very graphic demonstration of the problems we have been facing for the last two years.

I might start by saying that, with respect to Mr. Clapp's interpretation of the bill on issues of performance, exhibit, vending and rights other than photocopying, I'd refer you to the bill rather than to Mr. Clapp. I think Mr. Clapp knows that the Copyright Office has not been a tool of the publishing industry or of the "greedy" author interests of the United States. Our effort for fifteen years has been to try to arbitrate between the two camps, and I deplore the fact that there are separate camps and that they continue their hostilities.

The history of the photocopying problem in copyright law revision has been an interesting one. In about 1961, we began a process of sending out drafts of provisions, and these went through a painful evaluation process. As Mr. Clapp very well knows, the first draft that the Copyright Office put forward contained a provision that attempted in very explicit terms to come to grips with this problem. It was shot down as effectively as anything could possibly be shot down by the representatives of the librarians' associations themselves. Neither side wanted it. They agreed publicly—this is in print—that it was better to rely on the doctrine of fair use with respect to library photocopying, so this provision was dropped out of the bill. This provision was Section 9 of our preliminary draft.

It stayed in that posture until the bill passed the House, whereupon interest on the part of the library community revived rather dramatically. This was not merely because the bill had passed the House but also because photocopying has increased so substantially. I don't have any intention of getting into the hassle on numbers. I think that everyone in this audience knows from personal experience what the situation is with respect to photocopying and what the prospects are. Whether or not there should be legislation is something that the Congress will decide, but the growth of the use of photocopying machines was something the library representatives have been very conscious of. I think this was one of the reasons why, at the midwinter meeting of the American Library Association in January, 1968, a provision was drafted that was an effort to try to put back into the bill something along the lines of our old Section 9. Well, that was pretty late in the day, but the Copyright Office, grinding its teeth a little, went forward again to try to work this out. We talked individually to representatives of the various factions of the library community and of the publishing community. We had to talk with six or eight different people on each side, separately and then together. I differ with Mr. Clapp as to the constructive or retrograde nature of these discussions; I think they carried us further along. It does seem rather discouraging to come here and have all the same things said as if these discussions had never taken place; but that's life.

I do find the discussion today discouraging and particularly when it is hinted that the Copyright Office is the tool of the publishing industry. I'd like to go into that because the issue has been raised. It seemed to us in the Copyright Office, and in the Library of Congress of which the Copyright Office is a part, that the librarians had a point. We wouldn't have put Section 9 in our preliminary draft if we didn't think the librarians had a point. I don't mean to press this, but I do think that Mr. Clapp is contradictory when he says that fair use doesn't have anything to do with photocopying. If that is true, then what are you doing now but infringing copyrights left and right? In any case, we took the initiative, went forward, tried to bring the parties together and went through six or eight drafts. The drafts looked in the direction of the library amendments but were an attempt at compromise. It seemed like a compromisable issue, and I still think it is. The situation did reach an impasse partly because of personality conflicts. The issue became irreconcilable because of an unwillingness to budge on either side.

The Office has not taken an official position on this issue since the latest series of discussions, but I'll give you my personal views. I don't think the bill as it's drafted goes far enough. As it's drafted, it provides, first of all, for fair use. It is intended that, under the fair use provision and without regard to section 108, the librarians may continue to do as they are doing now. Nothing that is legal that you are doing now would be illegal under the bill, and that has nothing to do with section 108. Section 108 is an extra added attraction. It is intended, first of all, to provide for replacement of damaged copies, for archival preservation and for the exemption of unsupervised copying machines.

Then we come to the issue concerning the copying that the library does for the user over and above fair use—in other words, over and above what is legal now. The bill, as it emerged from the Senate Judiciary Subcommittee, permits single copying, including copying of whole works, of anything that is out of print. As the bill was drafted, an "out-of-print" work would not include something available from outfits like University Microfilms. If it is available there, then you are not to provide a photocopy.

There is no secret that, personally, I would have preferred to see the bill go further. But this is not my decision, nor Mr. Clapp's, nor Mr. Karp's, nor Mr. Lieb's. It is Congress's decision, and the Subcommittee was unanimous on this issue. The Senate Subcommittee on Patents, Trademarks and Copyrights of the Judiciary Committee has reported the bill and has prepared a draft report which is not final and which may change. I have informal permission to read you the following passage, emphasizing that it is not yet an official legislative document:

> The amendment proposed by the library associations would have authorized a library or archives to make at the request of a user a copy of a work provided it was for the personal use of the customer. The amendment would have permitted a library to furnish one

copy of even an entire work to each user who made such a request. The amendment was vigorously opposed by authors, publishers and by others who contend that it would authorize virtually unlimited copying and jeopardize scholarship by destroying the incentive for authors and publishers to produce new works. While the committee is sympathetic to the desire of libraries to provide services to their customers, the proposed amendment was more sweeping than is necessary for the satisfaction of the research needs of library users. Other than for the specific exemptions enumerated in subsections (b), (c), and (d), the scope of permissible copying by libraries and archives should be determined by section 107.

Library copying must be judged a fair use or an infringement on the basis of all of the relevant criteria and the facts of a particular situation. While it is not possible to formulate rules of general application, the making of a single copy of an article in a periodical or a short excerpt from a book would normally be regarded as fair use.

The Senate has previously determined by the passage of S.2216 of the 90th Congress that the copyright implications of the reproduction of copyrighted works by various forms of machine reproduction, including library copying, should be one of the issues to be studied by the National Commission on New Technological Uses of Copyrighted Works. Since the current needs of scholarship and research are adequately recognized in sections 107 and 108, any major innovations in reprography policy should await the studies and report of the Commission.

The library associations have expressed concern that the failure of the Congress to accept all of the provisions of their proposed amendment might be interpreted as reflecting a disposition to narrow rights of reproduction authorized by the existing Copyright Act. Nothing in this bill or its legislative history should be interpreted as reflecting an intention of the Congress to reduce the right of libraries to reproduce copyrighted works.

> Any reproduction authorized by the Act of 1909 will continue to be authorized under this legislation.

The thrust of this is that you are gaining, not losing, under Section 108. Now the question that is very relevant is whether you are gaining enough. After the bill was reported, the issue was discussed at a meeting of the A.L.A., and a position was adopted that would accept 108 with an amendment. The crux of the amendment, as I would interpret it, is to relieve the librarian of policing authority. It is intended to place the responsibility on the user rather than the library—to insulate the librarian and the library from liability where reasonable differences could exist as to whether something is fair use or not. Speaking personally, I believe that this is a viable principle. The language that was adopted was not acceptable to the authors and publishers for reasons already explained. They feel that, to coin a phrase, it throws the baby out with the bath water. I am not so sure that the underlying principle is unacceptable to them, and I think a formula can be found that meets both sides of this issue.

I must say, however, that if we continue to have these confrontations, we're not going to get anywhere.

MR. CLAPP: I want to assure you and Miss Ringer that I did not intend to accuse her and the Copyright Office of being a tool of the publishing industry. If it has been interpreted that way, I hastily withdraw it and offer you my apology. These opinions which are found in the Copyright Office and register's recommendations on the bill certainly appear to an unfriendly eye to be in the service of the publishers. But that is something else again. This does not impute a motive. I withdraw and completely deny any imputation of motives here.

As for the meetings I spoke of and which Miss Ringer has spoken of, I wish to underscore what she has said and tell you that she personally has had her head badly bloodied in the course of the discussions, and my heart has bled for her.

Finally, that retraction that she has read us—that draft report, the subcommittee report—completely sustains the impression that I gained from the speakers this morning, namely, the committee is talking about two different things in Section 107 and Section 108. They are talking about what we call normal photocopying practice in 107. But instead of telling us so that we may engage in it, they tell us that if we continue to engage in it, these are the criteria which a court of law will invoke in order to find out whether we are in infringement or not. It's a heck of a thing, if I may so so, to tell 30,000 public service agencies which are doing their darndest to serve the public, "You seem to be doing okay, go ahead and do it, and if you are sued, here are the criteria by which you will be adjudged." There is absolutely nothing in any law or case or statute, Miss Ringer, to say that copying of an article is fair use photocopying. There is absolutely nothing. Now, if this is good enough to put into a report, then it is good enough to put into a statute.

MR. KARP: Sometimes I think that the dramatic content of some people's lives is a little impoverished, because you would think there was a tremendous battle going on, while it was pretty dull, cut and dry and a lot of nonsense. Nobody's head was bloodied and nobody's heart bled. What really indicates whose tool the Copyright Office is are the cases where something was really at stake. In two or three cases that I am most concerned about, it was the authors against the Copyright Office, fighting vigorously over an interpretation of the manufacturing clause which would gut the rights of hundreds of American authors. One case involved a novel called *Candy*. The Copyright Office took a view of the manufacturing clause which destroyed the right of the two authors of this novel. They weren't paid a single penny of royalty on hundreds of thousands of copies. Now if you want to talk about tools, that is where it counts—in the pocketbook. And if you want to look at whose friends are whose, you can rest assured that the Copyright Office is not always a friend of American authors, not by a long shot.

As far as the particular provisions of Section 107 and 108 are concerned, how do you write legislation? Mr. Clapp comes to us with an entirely new approach. I guess he wants something conversational, something out of the Psalms such as, "These are the blessed, they may do as follows." We don't write laws like this. The bill says fair use is permitted and here are the criteria. In an area where definition is vague, you can't start writing that six pages from the *Saturday Review* is fair use, but if you go beyond forty-seven pages from a novel which is 300 pages long, it is not fair use, ...

PART IV

Appendix 1

Copyright Law of the United States of America

Copyright Law

OF THE

UNITED STATES OF AMERICA

Copyright Office Application Forms

The Copyright Office has prepared forms for use in applying for the registration of claims to copyright in works included in classes (a) through (m) which are found in section 5 of the copyright law (Title 17, United States Code) appearing on pages 4 and 5 of this bulletin. These application forms, listed below, are supplied free upon request. State the form for which you have a need and address your communication to: Register of Copyrights, Library of Congress, Washington, D.C. 20540.

Class A   Form A—Published book manufactured in the United States of America.

Class A or B

Form A–B Foreign—Book or periodical manufactured outside the United States of America (except works subject to the ad interim provisions of the copyright law).

Form A–B Ad Interim—Book or periodical in the English language manufactured and first published outside the United States of America.

Class B

Form B—Periodical manufactured in the United States of America.

Form BB—Contribution to a periodical manufactured in the United States of America.

Class C   Form C—Lecture or similar production prepared for oral delivery.

Class D   Form D—Dramatic or dramatico-musical composition.

Class E

Form E—Musical composition the author of which is a citizen or domiciliary of the United States of America or which was first published in the United States of America.

Form E Foreign—Musical composition the author of which is not a citizen or domiciliary of the United States of America and which was not first published in the United States of America.

Class F   Form F—Map.

Class G   Form G—Work of art or a model or design for a work of art.

Class H   Form H—Reproduction of a work of art.

Class I   Form I—Drawing or plastic work of a scientific or technical character.

Class J   Form J—Photograph.

Class K

Form K—Print or pictorial illustration.

Form KK—Print or label used for an article of merchandise.

Class L or M

Form L–M—Motion picture.

Form R—Renewal copyright.

Form U—Notice of use of copyrighted music on mechanical instruments.

Copyright Law

OF THE

UNITED STATES OF AMERICA

Bulletin No. 14

(Revised to July 1, 1969)

COPYRIGHT OFFICE

LIBRARY OF CONGRESS

Washington, D.C.   20540

1969

For sale by the Superintendent of Documents, U.S. Government Printing Office
Washington, D.C. 20402 - Price 45 cents

Prefatory Note

The Copyright Law of the United States printed herein is Title 17 of the United States Code, as codified and enacted into positive law by the Act of July 30, 1947 (61 Stat. 652) and amended by the Act of April 27, 1948 (62 Stat. 202), effective thirty days after its enactment; the Act of June 25, 1948 (62 Stat. 869), effective September 1, 1948; the Act of June 3, 1949 (63 Stat. 153); the Act of October 31, 1951 (65 Stat. 710); the Act of July 17, 1952 (66 Stat. 752), effective January 1, 1953; the Act of April 13, 1954 (68 Stat. 52); and the Act of August 31, 1954 (68 Stat. 1030), which became effective upon the coming into force of the Universal Copyright Convention on September 16, 1955.   The Copyright Law was further amended by the Act of March 29, 1956 (70 Stat. 63); by the Act of September 7, 1957 (71 Stat. 633), effective one year after the date of enactment; by the Act of September 7, 1962 (76 Stat. 442), effective November 1, 1962; and by the Act of October 27, 1965 (79 Stat. 1072), effective thirty days after its enactment.   In addition, there were four acts extending the duration of copyright protection in certain cases: the Act of September 19, 1962 (76 Stat. 555); the Act of August 28, 1965 (79 Stat. 581); the Act of November 16, 1967 (81 Stat. 464); and the Act of July 23, 1968 (82 Stat. 397).   The basic Act was that of March 4, 1909, as amended.   The substance of that Act is contained in the Act of July 30, 1947, with changes in form and in the arrangement and numbering of the sections.   Parallel reference tables showing disposition of sections of the Act of March 4, 1909, as amended, in Title 17, United States Code, are on page 29.

L. C. card 12–35200

Contents

The Constitutional Provision Respecting Copyright

The Congress shall have Power . . . To promote the Progress of Science and useful Arts, by securing for limited Times to Authors and Inventors the exclusive Right to their respective Writings and Discoveries. (U.S. Const. Art. I, § 8)

Copyright Law

OF THE UNITED STATES OF AMERICA

United States Code

Title 17—Copyrights [1]

CHAPTER 1—Registration of Copyrights

---

[1] Act of July 30, 1947 (61 Stat. 652). The enacting clause provides that Title 17 of the United States Code entitled "Copyrights" is codified and enacted into positive law and may be cited as "Title 17, U. S. C. § —". The Act of April 27, 1948 (62 Stat. 202) amended sections 211 and 215. The Act of June 25, 1948 (62 Stat. 869) repealed sections 101 (f), 102, 103, 110 and 111; however, see sections 1338, 1400, 1498 (b, c) and 2072 (Title 28, United States Code) appearing on pages 33–35 of this bulletin and the Federal Rules of Civil Procedure. The Act of June 3, 1949 (63 Stat. 153) amended sections 16, 22, 23 and 215 as well as section 22 of the analysis of chapter 1. The Act of October 31, 1951 (65 Stat. 710) amended sections 3, 8, 112 and 114, and struck out the items of the analysis of chapter 2 relating to the repealed sections. The Act of July 17, 1952 (66 Stat. 752) amended section 1 (c). The Act of April 13, 1954 (68 Stat. 52) added section 216 and amended the analysis of chapter 3. The Act of August 31, 1954 (68 Stat. 1030) amended sections 9, 16 and 19. The Act of March 29, 1956 (70 Stat. 63) amended section 13. The Act of September 7, 1957 (71 Stat. 633) amended section 115. The Act of September 7, 1962 (76 Stat. 442) amended the first paragraph of section 8. The Acts of September 19, 1962 (76 Stat. 555), August 28, 1965 (79 Stat. 581), November 16, 1967 (81 Stat. 464), and July 23, 1968 (82 Stat. 397) extended the duration of copyright protection in certain cases under section 24. The Act of October 27, 1965 (79 Stat. 1072) amended sections 211 and 215.

§ 1. EXCLUSIVE RIGHTS AS TO COPYRIGHTED WORKS.—Any person entitled thereto, upon complying with the provisions of this title, shall have the exclusive right:

(a) To print, reprint, publish, copy, and vend the copyrighted work;

(b) To translate the copyrighted work into other languages or dialects, or make any other version thereof, if it be a literary work; to dramatize it if it be a nondramatic work; to convert it into a novel or other nondramatic work if it be a drama; to arrange or adapt it if it be a musical work; to complete, execute, and finish it if it be a model or design for a work of art;

(c) [1] To deliver, authorize the delivery of, read, or present the copyrighted work in public for profit if it be a lecture, sermon, address or similar production, or other nondramatic literary work; to make or procure the making of any transcription or record thereof by or from which, in whole or in part, it may in any manner or by any method be exhibited, delivered, presented, produced, or reproduced; and to play or perform it in public for profit, and to exhibit, represent, produce, or reproduce it in any manner or by any method whatsoever. The damages for the infringement by broadcast of any work referred to in this subsection shall not exceed the sum of $100 where the infringing broadcaster shows

---

[1] Section 1 (c) as amended by the Act of July 17, 1952 (66 Stat. 752), effective January 1, 1953.

that he was not aware that he was infringing and that such infringement could not have been reasonably foreseen; and

(d) To perform or represent the copyrighted work publicly if it be a drama or, if it be a dramatic work and not reproduced in copies for sale, to vend any manuscript or any record whatsoever thereof; to make or to procure the making of any transcription or record thereof by or from which, in whole or in part, it may in any manner or by any method be exhibited, performed, represented, produced, or reproduced; and to exhibit, perform, represent, produce, or reproduce it in any manner or by any method whatsoever; and

(e) To perform the copyrighted work publicly for profit if it be a musical composition; and for the purpose of public performance for profit, and for the purposes set forth in subsection (a) hereof, to make any arrangement or setting of it or of the melody of it in any system of notation or any form of record in which the thought of an author may be recorded and from which it may be read or reproduced: *Provided,* That the provisions of this title, so far as they secure copyright controlling the parts of instruments serving to reproduce mechanically the musical work, shall include only compositions published and copyrighted after July 1, 1909, and shall not include the works of a foreign author or composer unless the foreign state or nation of which such author or composer is a citizen or subject grants, either by treaty, convention, agreement, or law, to citizens of the United States similar rights. And as a condition of extending the copyright control to such mechanical reproductions, that whenever the owner of a musical copyright has used or permitted or knowingly acquiesced in the use of the copyrighted work upon the parts of instruments serving to reproduce mechanically the musical work, any other person may make similar use of the copyrighted work upon the payment to the copyright proprietor of a royalty of 2 cents on each such part manufactured, to be paid by the manufacturer thereof; and the copyright proprietor may require, and if so the manufacturer shall furnish, a report under oath on the 20th day of each month on the number of parts of instruments manufactured during the previous month serving to reproduce mechanically said musical work, and royalties shall be due on the parts manufactured during any month upon the 20th of the next succeeding month. The payment of the royalty provided for by this section shall free the articles or devices for which such royalty has been paid from further contribution to the copyright except in case of public performance for profit. It shall be the duty of the copyright owner, if he uses the musical composition himself for the manufacture of parts of instruments serving to reproduce mechanically the musical work, or licenses others to do so, to file notice thereof, accompanied by a recording fee, in the copyright office, and any failure to file such notice shall be a complete defense to any suit, action, or proceeding for any infringement of such copyright.

In case of failure of such manufacturer to pay to the copyright proprietor within thirty days after demand in writing the full sum of royalties due at said rate at the date of such demand, the court may award taxable costs to the plaintiff and a reasonable counsel fee, and the court may, in its discretion, enter judgment therein for any sum in addition over the amount found to be due as royalty in accordance with the terms of this title, not exceeding three times such amount.

The reproduction or rendition of a musical composition by or upon coin-operated machines shall not be deemed a public performance for profit unless a fee is charged for admission to the place where such reproduction or rendition occurs.

§ 2. RIGHTS OF AUTHOR OR PROPRIETOR OF UNPUBLISHED WORK. —Nothing in this title shall be construed to annul or limit the right of the author or proprietor of an unpublished work, at common law or in equity, to prevent the copying, publication, or use of such unpublished work without his consent, and to obtain damages therefor.

§ 3. PROTECTION OF COMPONENT PARTS OF WORK COPYRIGHTED; COMPOSITE WORKS OR PERIODICALS.—The copyright provided by this title shall protect all the copyrightable component parts of the work copyrighted, and all matter therein in which copyright is already subsisting, but without extending the duration or scope of such copyright.   The copyright upon composite works or periodicals shall give to the proprietor thereof all the rights in respect thereto which he would have if each part were individually copyrighted under this title.

§ 4. ALL WRITINGS OF AUTHOR INCLUDED.—The works for which copyright may be secured under this title shall include all the writings of an author.

§ 5. CLASSIFICATION OF WORKS FOR REGISTRATION.—The application for registration shall specify to which of the following classes the work in which copyright is claimed belongs:

(a) Books, including composite and cyclopedic works, directories, gazetteers, and other compilations.

(b) Periodicals, including newspapers.

(c) Lectures, sermons, addresses (prepared for oral delivery).

(d) Dramatic or dramatico-musical compositions.

(e) Musical compositions.

(f) Maps.

(g) Works of art; models or designs for works of art.

(h) Reproductions of a work of art.

(i) Drawings or plastic works of a scientific or technical character.

(j) Photographs.

(k) Prints and pictorial illustrations including prints or labels used for articles of merchandise.

(l) Motion-picture photoplays.

(m) Motion pictures other than photoplays.

The above specifications shall not be held to limit the subject matter of copyright as defined in section 4 of this title, nor shall any error in classification invalidate or impair the copyright protection secured under this title.

§ 6. REGISTRATION OF PRINTS AND LABELS.—Commencing July 1, 1940, the Register of Copyrights is charged with the registration of claims to copyright properly presented, in all prints and labels published in connection with the sale or advertisement of articles of merchandise, including all claims to copyright in prints and labels pending in the Patent Office and uncleared at the close of business June 30, 1940. There shall be paid for registering a claim of copyright in any such print or label not a trade-mark $6, which sum shall cover the expense of furnishing a certificate of such registration, under the seal of the Copyright Office, to the claimant of copyright.

§ 7. COPYRIGHT ON COMPILATIONS OF WORKS IN PUBLIC DOMAIN OR OF COPYRIGHTED WORKS; SUBSISTING COPYRIGHTS NOT AFFECTED.—Compilations or abridgments, adaptations, arrangements, dramatizations, translations, or other versions of works in the public domain or of copyrighted works when produced with the consent of the proprietor of the copyright in such works, or works republished with new matter, shall be regarded as new works subject to copyright under the provisions of this title; but the publication of any such new works shall not affect the force or validity of any subsisting copyright upon the matter employed or any part thereof, or be construed to imply an exclusive right to such use of the original works, or to secure or extend copyright in such original works.

§ 8. COPYRIGHT NOT TO SUBSIST IN WORKS IN PUBLIC DOMAIN, OR PUBLISHED PRIOR TO JULY 1, 1909, AND NOT ALREADY COPYRIGHTED, OR GOVERNMENT PUBLICATIONS; PUBLICATION BY GOVERNMENT OF COPYRIGHTED MATERIAL.[1]—No copyright shall subsist in

---

[1] Section 8 as amended by the Act of September 7, 1962 (76 Stat. 442, at 446), effective November 1, 1962.

the original text of any work which is in the public domain, or in any work which was published in this country or any foreign country prior to July 1, 1909, and has not been already copyrighted in the United States, or in any publication of the United States Government, or any reprint, in whole or in part, thereof, except that the Postmaster General may secure copyright on behalf of the United States in the whole or any part of the publications authorized by section 2506 of title 39.[1]

The publication or republication by the Government, either separately or in a public document, of any material in which copyright is subsisting shall not be taken to cause any abridgment or annulment of the copyright or to authorize any use or appropriation of such copyright material without the consent of the copyright proprietor.

§ 9. AUTHORS OR PROPRIETORS, ENTITLED: ALIENS.[2]—The author or proprietor of any work made the subject of copyright by this title, or his executors, administrators, or assigns, shall have copyright for such work under the conditions and for the terms specified in this title: *Provided, however,* That the copyright secured by this title shall extend to the work of an author or proprietor who is a citizen or subject of a foreign state or nation only under the conditions described in subsections (a), (b), or (c) below:

(a) When an alien author or proprietor shall be domiciled within the United States at the time of the first publication of his work; or

(b) When the foreign state or nation of which such author or proprietor is a citizen or subject grants, either by treaty, convention, agreement, or law, to citizens of the United States the benefit of copyright on substantially the same basis as to its own citizens, or copyright protection, substantially equal to the protection secured to such foreign author under this title or by treaty; or when such foreign state or nation is a party to an international agreement which provides for reciprocity in the granting of copyright, by the terms of which agreement the United States may, at its pleasure, become a party thereto.

The existence of the reciprocal conditions aforesaid shall be determined by the President of the United States, by proclamation made from time to time, as the purposes of this title may require:

---

[1] A further exception was provided by a statute enacted in 1968 (82 Stat. 339, 340) amending Title 15 of the U.S. Code (15 U.S.C. 272), authorizing the Secretary of Commerce at § 290 (e) "to secure copyright and renewal thereof on behalf of the United States as author or proprietor in all or any part of any standard reference data which he prepares or makes available under this chapter, and may authorize the reproduction and publication thereof by others."

[a] Section 9 as amended by the Act of August 31, 1954 (68 Stat. 1030), effective upon the coming into force of the Universal Copyright Convention in the United States of America. (The Universal Copyright Convention came into force on September 16, 1955.)

Provided, That whenever the President shall find that the authors, copyright owners, or proprietors of works first produced or published abroad and subject to copyright or to renewal of copyright under the laws of the United States, including works subject to ad interim copyright, are or may have been temporarily unable to comply with the conditions and formalities prescribed with respect to such works by the copyright laws of the United States, because of the disruption or suspension of facilities essential for such compliance, he may by proclamation grant such extension of time as he may deem appropriate for the fulfillment of such conditions or formalities by authors, copyright owners, or proprietors who are citizens of the United States or who are nationals of countries which accord substantially equal treatment in this respect to authors, copyright owners, or proprietors who are citizens of the United States: *Provided further,* That no liability shall attach under this title for lawful uses made or acts done prior to the effective date of such proclamation in connection with such works, or in respect to the continuance for one year subsequent to such date of any business undertaking or enterprise lawfully undertaken prior to such date involving expenditure or contractual obligation in connection with the exploitation, production, reproduction, circulation, or performance of any such work.

The President may at any time terminate any proclamation authorized herein or any part thereof or suspend or extend its operation for such period or periods of time as in his judgment the interests of the United States may require.

(c) When the Universal Copyright Convention, signed at Geneva on September 6, 1952, shall be in force [1] between the United States of America and the foreign state or nation of which such author is a citizen or subject, or in which the work was first published. Any work to which copyright is extended pursuant to this subsection shall be exempt from the following provisions of this title: (1) The requirement in section 1 (e) that a foreign state or nation must grant to United States citizens mechanical reproduction rights similar to those specified therein; (2) the obligatory deposit requirements of the first sentence of section 13; (3) the provisions of sections 14, 16, 17, and 18; (4) the import prohibitions of section 107, to the extent that they are related to the manufacturing requirements of section 16; and (5) the requirements of sections 19 and 20: *Provided, however,* That such exemptions shall apply only if from the time of first publication all the copies of the work published with the authority of the author or other copyright proprietor shall bear the symbol ©

---

[1] The Universal Copyright Convention came into force in the United States of America on September 16, 1955. For text, see pages 43–55, *infra.*

accompanied by the name of the copyright proprietor and the year of first publication placed in such manner and location as to give reasonable notice of claim of copyright.

Upon the coming into force of the Universal Copyright Convention in a foreign state or nation as hereinbefore provided, every book or periodical of a citizen or subject thereof in which ad interim copyright was subsisting on the effective date of said coming into force shall have copyright for twenty-eight years from the date of first publication abroad without the necessity of complying with the further formalities specified in section 23 of this title.

The provisions of this subsection shall not be extended to works of an author who is a citizen of, or domiciled in the United States of America regardless of place of first publication, or to works first published in the United States.

§ 10. PUBLICATION OF WORK WITH NOTICE.—Any person entitled thereto by this title may secure copyright for his work by publication thereof with the notice of copyright required by this title; and such notice shall be affixed to each copy thereof published or offered for sale in the United States by authority of the copyright proprietor, except in the case of books seeking ad interim protection under section 22 of this title.

§ 11. REGISTRATION OF CLAIM AND ISSUANCE OF CERTIFICATE.— Such person may obtain registration of his claim to copyright by complying with the provisions of this title, including the deposit of copies, and upon such compliance the Register of Copyrights shall issue to him the certificates provided for in section 209 of this title.

§ 12. WORKS NOT REPRODUCED FOR SALE.—Copyright may also be had of the works of an author, of which copies are not reproduced for sale, by the deposit, with claim of copyright, of one complete copy of such work if it be a lecture or similar production or a dramatic, musical, or dramatico-musical composition; of a title and description, with one print taken from each scene or act, if the work be a motion-picture photoplay; of a photographic print if the work be a photograph; of a title and description, with not less than two prints taken from different sections of a complete motion picture, if the work be a motion picture other than a photoplay; or of a photograph or other identifying reproduction thereof, if it be a work of art or a plastic work or drawing. But the privilege of registration of copyright secured hereunder shall not exempt the copyright proprietor from the deposit of copies, under sections 13 and 14 of this title, where the work is later reproduced in copies for sale.

§ 13. DEPOSIT OF COPIES AFTER PUBLICATION; ACTION OR PROCEEDING FOR INFRINGEMENT.[1]—After copyright has been secured by publication of the work with the notice of copyright as provided in section 10 of this title, there shall be promptly deposited in the Copyright Office or in the mail addressed to the Register of Copyrights, Washington, District of Columbia, two complete copies of the best edition thereof then published, or if the work is by an author who is a citizen or subject of a foreign state or nation and has been published in a foreign country, one complete copy of the best edition then published in such foreign country, which copies or copy, if the work be a book or periodical, shall have been produced in accordance with the manufacturing provisions specified in section 16 of this title; or if such work be a contribution to a periodical, for which contribution special registration is requested, one copy of the issue or issues containing such contribution; or if the work belongs to a class specified in subsections (g), (h), (i) or (k) of section 5 of this title, and if the Register of Copyrights determines that it is impracticable to deposit copies because of their size, weight, fragility, or monetary value he may permit the deposit of photographs or other identifying reproductions in lieu of copies of the work as published under such rules and regulations as he may prescribe with the approval of the Librarian of Congress; or if the work is not reproduced in copies for sale there shall be deposited the copy, print, photograph, or other identifying reproduction provided by section 12 of this title, such copies or copy, print, photograph, or other reproduction to be accompanied in each case by a claim of copyright. No action or proceeding shall be maintained for infringement of copyright in any work until the provisions of this title with respect to the deposit of copies and registration of such work shall have been complied with.

§ 14. SAME; FAILURE TO DEPOSIT; DEMAND; PENALTY.—Should the copies called for by section 13 of this title not be promptly deposited as provided in this title, the Register of Copyrights may at any time after the publication of the work, upon actual notice, require the proprietor of the copyright to deposit them, and after the said demand shall have been made, in default of the deposit of copies of the work within three months from any part of the United States, except an outlying territorial possession of the United States, or within six months from any outlying territorial possession of the United States, or from any foreign country, the proprietor of the copyright shall be liable to a fine of $100 and to

---

[1] Section 13 as amended by the Act of March 29, 1956 (70 Stat. 63).

pay to the Library of Congress twice the amount of the retail price of the best edition of the work, and the copyright shall become void.

§ 15. SAME; POSTMASTER'S RECEIPT; TRANSMISSION BY MAIL WITHOUT COST.—The postmaster to whom are delivered the articles deposited as provided in sections 12 and 13 of this title shall, if requested, give a receipt therefor and shall mail them to their destination without cost to the copyright claimant.

§ 16. MECHANICAL WORK TO BE DONE IN UNITED STATES.[1]—Of the printed book or periodical specified in section 5, subsections (a) and (b), of this title, except the original text of a book or periodical of foreign origin in a language or languages other than English, the text of all copies accorded protection under this title, except as below provided, shall be printed from type set within the limits of the United States, either by hand or by the aid of any kind of typesetting machine, or from plates made within the limits of the United States from type set therein, or, if the text be produced by lithographic process, or photoengraving process, then by a process wholly performed within the limits of the United States, and the printing of the text and binding of the said book shall be performed within the limits of the United States; which requirements shall extend also to the illustrations within a book consisting of printed text and illustrations produced by lithographic process, or photoengraving process, and also to separate lithographs or photoengravings, except where in either case the subjects represented are located in a foreign country and illustrate a scientific work or reproduce a work of art: *Provided, however,* That said requirements shall not apply to works in raised characters for the use of the blind, or to books or periodicals of foreign origin in a language or languages other than English, or to works printed or produced in the United States by any other process than those above specified in this section, or to copies of books or periodicals, first published abroad in the English language, imported into the United States within five years after first publication in a foreign state or nation up to the number of fifteen hundred copies of each such book or periodical if said copies shall contain notice of copyright in accordance with sections 10, 19, and 20 of this title and if ad interim copyright in said work shall have been obtained pursuant to section 22 of this title prior to the importation into the United States of any copy except those permitted by the provisions of section 107 of this title: *Provided further,* That the provisions of this section shall not affect the right of importation under the provisions of section 107 of this title.

§ 17. AFFIDAVIT TO ACCOMPANY COPIES.—In the case of the book the copies so deposited shall be accompanied by an affidavit under the official seal of any officer authorized to administer oaths within the United States, duly made by the person claiming copyright or by his duly authorized agent or representative residing in the United States, or by the printer who has printed the book, setting forth that the copies deposited have been printed from type set within the limits of the United States or from plates made within the limits of the United States from type set therein; or, if the text be produced by lithographic process, or photoengraving process, that such process was wholly performed within the limits of the United States and that the printing of the text and binding of the said book have also been performed within the limits of the United States. Such affidavit shall state also the place where and the establishment or establishments in which such type was set or plates made or lithographic process, or photoengraving process or printing and binding were performed and the date of the completion of the printing of the book or the date of publication.

§ 18. MAKING FALSE AFFIDAVIT.—Any person who, for the purpose of obtaining registration of a claim to copyright, shall knowingly make a false affidavit as to his having complied with the above conditions shall be deemed guilty of a misdemeanor, and upon conviction thereof shall be punished by a fine of not more than $1,000, and all of his rights and privileges under said copyright shall thereafter be forfeited.

§ 19. NOTICE; FORM.[1]—The notice of copyright required by section 10 of this title shall consist either of the word "Copyright", the abbreviation "Copr.", or the symbol ©, accompanied by the name of the copyright proprietor, and if the work be a printed literary, musical, or dramatic work, the notice shall include also the year in which the copyright was secured by publication. In the case, however, of copies of works specified in subsections (f) to (k), inclusive, of section 5 of this title, the notice may consist of the letter C enclosed within a circle, thus ©, accompanied by the initials, monogram, mark, or symbol of the copyright proprietor: *Provided,* That on some accessible portion of such copies or of the margin, back, permanent base, or pedestal, or of the substance on which such copies shall be mounted, his name shall

---

[1] Section 19 as amended by the Act of August 31, 1954 (68 Stat. 1030), effective upon the coming into force of the Universal Copyright Convention in the United States of America (i.e., September 16, 1955).

appear.   But in the case of works in which copyright was subsisting on July 1, 1909, the notice of copyright may be either in one of the forms prescribed herein or may consist of the following words: "Entered according to Act of Congress, in the year by A. B., in the office of the Librarian of Congress, at Washington, D. C.," or, at his option, the word "Copyright", together with the year the copyright was entered and the name of the party by whom it was taken out; thus, "Copyright, 19—, by A. B."

§ 20. SAME; PLACE OF APPLICATION OF; ONE NOTICE IN EACH VOLUME OR NUMBER OF NEWSPAPER OR PERIODICAL.—The notice of copyright shall be applied, in the case of a book or other printed publication, upon its title page or the page immediately following, or if a periodical either upon the title page or upon the first page of text of each separate number or under the title heading, or if a musical work either upon its title page or the first page of music. One notice of copyright in each volume or in each number of a newspaper or periodical published shall suffice.

§ 21. SAME; EFFECT OF ACCIDENTAL OMISSION FROM COPY OR COPIES.—Where the copyright proprietor has sought to comply with the provisions of this title with respect to notice, the omission by accident or mistake of the prescribed notice from a particular copy or copies shall not invalidate the copyright or prevent recovery for infringement against any person who, after actual notice of the copyright, begins an undertaking to infringe it, but shall prevent the recovery of damages against an innocent infringer who has been misled by the omission of the notice; and in a suit for infringement no permanent injunction shall be had unless the copyright proprietor shall reimburse to the innocent infringer his reasonable outlay innocently incurred if the court, in its discretion, shall so direct.

§ 22. AD INTERIM PROTECTION OF BOOK OR PERIODICAL PUBLISHED ABROAD.[1]—In the case of a book or periodical first published abroad in the English language, the deposit in the Copyright Office, not later than six months after its publication abroad, of one complete copy of the foreign edition, with a request for the reservation of the copyright and a statement of the name and nationality of the author and of the copyright proprietor and of the date of publication of the said book or periodical, shall secure to the author or proprietor an ad interim copyright therein, which shall have all the force and effect given to copyright by this title, and shall endure until the expiration of five years after the date of first publication abroad.

---

[1] Section 22 as amended by the Act of June 3, 1949 (63 Stat. 153).

§ 23. SAME; EXTENSION TO FULL TERM.[1]—Whenever within the period of such ad interim protection an authorized edition of such books or periodicals shall be published within the United States, in accordance with the manufacturing provisions specified in section 16 of this title, and whenever the provisions of this title as to deposit of copies, registration, filing of affidavits, and the printing of the copyright notice shall have been duly complied with, the copyright shall be extended to endure in such book or periodical for the term provided in this title.

§ 24. DURATION; RENEWAL AND EXTENSION.[2]—The copyright secured by this title shall endure for twenty-eight years from the date of first publication, whether the copyrighted work bears the author's true name or is published anonymously or under an assumed name: *Provided,* That in the case of any posthumous work or of any periodical, cyclopedic, or other composite work upon which the copyright was originally secured by the proprietor thereof, or of any work copyrighted by a corporate body (otherwise than as assignee or licensee of the individual author) or by an employer for whom such work is made for hire, the proprietor of such copyright shall be entitled to a renewal and extension of the copyright in such work for the further term of twenty-eight years when application for such renewal and extension shall have been made to the copyright office and duly registered therein within one year prior to the expiration of the original term of copyright: *And provided further,* That in the case of any other copyrighted work, including a contribution by an individual author to a periodical or to a cyclopedic or other composite work, the author of such work, if still living, or the widow, widower, or children of the author, if the author be not living, or if such author, widow, widower, or children be not living, then the author's executors, or in the absence of a will, his next of kin shall be entitled to a renewal and extension of the copyright in such work for a further term of twenty-eight years when application for such renewal and extension shall have been made to the copyright office and duly registered therein within one year prior to the expiration of the original term of copyright: *And provided further,* That in default of the registration of such application for renewal and extension, the copyright in any work shall determine at the expiration of twenty-eight years from first publication.

§ 25. RENEWAL OF COPYRIGHTS REGISTERED IN PATENT OFFICE

---

[1] Section 23 as amended by the Act of June 3, 1949 (63 Stat. 153).
[2] Four acts extending the duration of copyright protection in certain cases relate to section 24: the Act of September 19, 1962 (76 Stat. 555), the Act of August 28, 1965 (79 Stat. 581), the Act of November 16, 1967 (81 Stat. 464), and the Act of July 23, 1968 (82 Stat. 397). (See Appendix, pages 31–32.)

UNDER REPEALED LAW.—Subsisting copyrights originally registered in the Patent Office prior to July 1, 1940, under section 3 of the act of June 18, 1874, shall be subject to renewal in behalf of the proprietor upon application made to the Register of Copyrights within one year prior to the expiration of the original term of twenty-eight years.

§ 26. TERMS DEFINED.—In the interpretation and construction of this title "the date of publication" shall in the case of a work of which copies are reproduced for sale or distribution be held to be the earliest date when copies of the first authorized edition were placed on sale, sold, or publicly distributed by the proprietor of the copyright or under his authority, and the word "author" shall include an employer in the case of works made for hire.

§ 27. COPYRIGHT DISTINCT FROM PROPERTY IN OBJECT COPYRIGHTED; EFFECT OF SALE OF OBJECT, AND OF ASSIGNMENT OF COPYRIGHT.—The copyright is distinct from the property in the material object copyrighted, and the sale or conveyance, by gift or otherwise, of the material object shall not of itself constitute a transfer of the copyright, nor shall the assignment of the copyright constitute a transfer of the title to the material object; but nothing in this title shall be deemed to forbid, prevent, or restrict the transfer of any copy of a copyrighted work the possession of which has been lawfully obtained.

§ 28. ASSIGNMENTS AND BEQUESTS.—Copyright secured under this title or previous copyright laws of the United States may be assigned, granted, or mortgaged by an instrument in writing signed by the proprietor of the copyright, or may be bequeathed by will.

§ 29. SAME; EXECUTED IN FOREIGN COUNTRY; ACKNOWLEDGMENT AND CERTIFICATE.—Every assignment of copyright executed in a foreign country shall be acknowledged by the assignor before a consular officer or secretary of legation of the United States authorized by law to administer oaths or perform notarial acts. The certificate of such acknowledgment under the hand and official seal of such consular officer or secretary of legation shall be prima facie evidence of the execution of the instrument.

§ 30. SAME; RECORD.—Every assignment of copyright shall be recorded in the copyright office within three calendar months after its execution in the United States or within six calendar months after its execution without the limits of the United States, in default of which it shall be void as against any subsequent purchaser or mortgagee for a valuable consideration, without notice, whose assignment has been duly recorded.

§ 31. SAME; CERTIFICATE OF RECORD.—The Register of Copyrights shall, upon payment of the prescribed fee, record such assignment, and shall return it to the sender with a certificate of record attached under seal of the copyright office, and upon the payment of the fee prescribed by this title he shall furnish to any person requesting the same a certified copy thereof under the said seal.

§ 32. SAME; USE OF NAME OF ASSIGNEE IN NOTICE.—When an assignment of the copyright in a specified book or other work has been recorded the assignee may substitute his name for that of the assignor in the statutory notice of copyright prescribed by this title.

CHAPTER 2—Infringement Proceedings [1]

§ 101. Infringement:
- (a) Injunction.
- (b) Damages and profits; amounts; other remedies.
- (c) Impounding during action.
- (d) Destruction of infringing copies and plates.
- (e) Royalties for use of mechanical reproduction of musical works.

§ 104. Willful infringement for profit.
§ 105. Fraudulent notice of copyright, or removal or alteration of notice.
§ 106. Importation of article bearing false notice or piratical copies of copyrighted work.
§ 107. Importation, during existence of copyright, of piratical copies, or of copies not produced in accordance with section 16 of this title.
§ 108. Forfeiture and destruction of articles prohibited importation.
§ 109. Importation of prohibited articles; regulations; proof of deposit of copies by complainants.
§ 112. Injunctions; service and enforcement.
§ 113. Transmission of certified copies of papers for enforcement of injunction by other court.
§ 114. Review of orders, judgments, or decrees.
§ 115. Limitations.
§ 116. Costs; attorney's fees.

§ 101. INFRINGEMENT.—If any person shall infringe the copyright in any work protected under the copyright laws of the United States such person shall be liable:

(a) INJUNCTION.—To an injunction restraining such infringement;

(b) DAMAGES AND PROFITS; AMOUNT; OTHER REMEDIES.—To

---

[1] Sections 101 (f), 102, 103, 110 and 111 were repealed by the Act of June 25, 1948 (62 Stat. 869, at 931, 936, 961 and 996), effective September 1, 1948. However, see sections 1338, 1400 and 2072, Title 28, United States Code, Appendix, pages 33–35, *infra*, and the Federal Rules of Civil Procedure, Appendix, pages 36–39, *infra*. Title 28 was amended by the Act of September 8, 1960 (74 Stat. 855), adding subsections (b) and (c) to section 1498, Appendix, *infra* at pages 33–34.

pay to the copyright proprietor such damages as the copyright proprietor may have suffered due to the infringement, as well as all the profits which the infringer shall have made from such infringement, and in proving profits the plaintiff shall be required to prove sales only, and the defendant shall be required to prove every element of cost which he claims, or in lieu of actual damages and profits, such damages as to the court shall appear to be just, and in assessing such damages the court may, in its discretion, allow the amounts as hereinafter stated, but in case of a newspaper reproduction of a copyrighted photograph, such damages shall not exceed the sum of $200 nor be less than the sum of $50, and in the case of the infringement of an undramatized or nondramatic work by means of motion pictures, where the infringer shall show that he was not aware that he was infringing, and that such infringement could not have been reasonably foreseen, such damages shall not exceed the sum of $100; and in the case of an infringement of a copyrighted dramatic or dramatico-musical work by a maker of motion pictures and his agencies for distribution thereof to exhibitors, where such infringer shows that he was not aware that he was infringing a copyrighted work, and that such infringements could not reasonably have been foreseen, the entire sum of such damages recoverable by the copyright proprietor from such infringing maker and his agencies for the distribution to exhibitors of such infringing motion picture shall not exceed the sum of $5,000 nor be less than $250, and such damages shall in no other case exceed the sum of $5,000 nor be less than the sum of $250, and shall not be regarded as a penalty. But the foregoing exceptions shall not deprive the copyright proprietor of any other remedy given him under this law, nor shall the limitation as to the amount of recovery apply to infringements occurring after the actual notice to a defendant, either by service of process in a suit or other written notice served upon him.

First. In the case of a painting, statue, or sculpture, $10 for every infringing copy made or sold by or found in the possession of the infringer or his agents or employees;

Second. In the case of any work enumerated in section 5 of this title, except a painting, statue, or sculpture, $1 for every infringing copy made or sold by or found in the possession of the infringer or his agents or employees;

Third. In the case of a lecture, sermon, or address, $50 for every infringing delivery;

Fourth. In the case of a dramatic or dramatico-musical or a choral or orchestral composition, $100 for the first and $50 for every subsequent infringing performance; in the case of other musical compositions $10 for every infringing performance;

(c) IMPOUNDING DURING ACTION.—To deliver up on oath, to be impounded during the pendency of the action, upon such terms and conditions as the court may prescribe, all articles alleged to infringe a copyright;

(d) DESTRUCTION OF INFRINGING COPIES AND PLATES.—To deliver up on oath for destruction all the infringing copies or devices, as well as all plates, molds, matrices, or other means for making such infringing copies as the court may order.

(e) ROYALTIES FOR USE OF MECHANICAL REPRODUCTION OF MUSICAL WORKS.—Whenever the owner of a musical copyright has used or permitted the use of the copyrighted work upon the parts of musical instruments serving to reproduce mechanically the musical work, then in case of infringement of such copyright by the unauthorized manufacture, use, or sale of interchangeable parts, such as disks, rolls, bands, or cylinders for use in mechanical music-producing machines adapted to reproduce the copyrighted music, no criminal action shall be brought, but in a civil action an injunction may be granted upon such terms as the court may impose, and the plaintiff shall be entitled to recover in lieu of profits and damages a royalty as provided in section 1, subsection (e), of this title: *Provided also,* That whenever any person, in the absence of a license agreement, intends to use a copyrighted musical composition upon the parts of instruments serving to reproduce mechanically the musical work, relying upon the compulsory license provision of this title, he shall serve notice of such intention, by registered mail, upon the copyright proprietor at his last address disclosed by the records of the copyright office, sending to the copyright office a duplicate of such notice; and in case of his failure so to do the court may, in its discretion, in addition to sums hereinabove mentioned, award the complainant a further sum, not to exceed three times the amount provided by section 1, subsection (e) of this title, by way of damages, and not as a penalty, and also a temporary injunction until the full award is paid.

[(f) See footnote 1, page 15, *supra.*]

[§ 102. See footnote 1, page 15, *supra.*]

[§ 103. See footnote 1, page 15, *supra.*]

§ 104. WILLFUL INFRINGEMENT FOR PROFIT.—Any person who willfully and for profit shall infringe any copyright secured by this title, or who shall knowingly and willfully aid or abet such infringement, shall be deemed guilty of a misdemeanor, and upon conviction thereof shall be punished by imprisonment for not exceeding one year or by a fine of not less than $100 nor more than $1,000, or both, in the discretion of the court: *Provided, however,* That nothing in this title shall be so construed as to prevent the performance of religious or secular works such as oratorios, cantatas, masses, or octavo choruses by public schools, church choirs, or vocal societies, rented, borrowed, or obtained from some public library, public school, church choir, school choir, or vocal society, provided the performance is given for charitable or educational purposes and not for profit.

§ 105. FRAUDULENT NOTICE OF COPYRIGHT, OR REMOVAL OR ALTERATION OF NOTICE.—Any person who, with fraudulent intent, shall insert or impress any notice of copyright required by this title, or words of the same purport, in or upon any uncopyrighted article, or with fraudulent intent shall remove or alter the copyright notice upon any article duly copyrighted shall be guilty of a misdemeanor, punishable by a fine of not less than $100 and not more than $1,000. Any person who shall knowingly issue or sell any article bearing a notice of United States copyright which has not been copyrighted in this country, or who shall knowingly import any article bearing such notice or words of the same purport, which has not been copyrighted in this country, shall be liable to a fine of $100.

§ 106. IMPORTATION OF ARTICLE BEARING FALSE NOTICE OR PIRATICAL COPIES OF COPYRIGHTED WORK.—The importation into the United States of any article bearing a false notice of copyright when there is no existing copyright thereon in the United States, or of any piratical copies of any work copyrighted in the United States, is prohibited.

§ 107. IMPORTATION, DURING EXISTENCE OF COPYRIGHT, OF PIRATICAL COPIES, OR OF COPIES NOT PRODUCED IN ACCORDANCE WITH SECTION 16 OF THIS TITLE.—During the existence of the American copyright in any book the importation into the United States of any piratical copies thereof or of any copies thereof (although authorized by the author or proprietor) which have not been produced in accordance with the manufacturing provisions specified in section 16 of this title, or any plates of the same not made from type set within the limits of the United States, or any copies thereof produced by lithographic or photoengraving process not performed within the limits of the United States, in accordance with the provisions of section 16 of this title, is prohibited: *Provided, however,* That, except as regards piratical copies, such prohibition shall not apply:

(a) To works in raised characters for the use of the blind.

(b) To a foreign newspaper or magazine, although containing

matter copyrighted in the United States printed or reprinted by authority of the copyright proprietor, unless such newspaper or magazine contains also copyright matter printed or reprinted without such authorization.

(c) To the authorized edition of a book in a foreign language or languages of which only a translation into English has been copyrighted in this country.

(d) To any book published abroad with the authorization of the author or copyright proprietor when imported under the circumstances stated in one of the four subdivisions following, that is to say:

First. When imported, not more than one copy at one time, for individual use and not for sale; but such privilege of importation shall not extend to a foreign reprint of a book by an American author copyrighted in the United States.

Second. When imported by the authority or for the use of the United States.

Third. When imported, for use and not for sale, not more than one copy of any such book in any one invoice, in good faith by or for any society or institution incorporated for educational, literary, philosophical, scientific or religious purposes, or for the encouragement of the fine arts, or for any college, academy, school, or seminary of learning, or for any State, school, college, university, or free public library in the United States.

Fourth. When such books form parts of libraries or collections purchased en bloc for the use of societies, institutions, or libraries designated in the foregoing paragraph, or form parts of the libraries or personal baggage belonging to persons or families arriving from foreign countries and are not intended for sale: *Provided,* That copies imported as above may not lawfully be used in any way to violate the rights of the proprietor of the American copyright or annul or limit the copyright protection secured by this title, and such unlawful use shall be deemed an infringement of copyright.

§ 108. FORFEITURE AND DESTRUCTION OF ARTICLES PROHIBITED IMPORTATION.—Any and all articles prohibited importation by this title which are brought into the United States from any foreign country (except in the mails) shall be seized and forfeited by like proceedings as those provided by law for the seizure and condemnation of property imported into the United States in violation of the customs revenue laws. Such articles when forfeited shall be destroyed in such manner as the Secretary of the Treasury or the court, as the case may be, shall direct: *Provided, however,* That all copies of authorized editions of copyright books imported in the mails or otherwise in violation of the provisions of this title may be exported and returned to the country of export whenever it is shown to the satisfaction of the Secretary of the Treasury, in a written application, that such importation does not involve willful negligence or fraud.

§ 109. IMPORTATION OF PROHIBITED ARTICLES; REGULATIONS; PROOF OF DEPOSIT OF COPIES BY COMPLAINANTS.—The Secretary of the Treasury and the Postmaster General are hereby empowered and required to make and enforce individually or jointly such rules and regulations as shall prevent the importation into the United States of articles prohibited importation by this title, and may require, as conditions precedent to exclusion of any work in which copyright is claimed, the copyright proprietor or any person claiming actual or potential injury by reason of actual or contemplated importations of copies of such work to file with the Post Office Department or the Treasury Department a certificate of the Register of Copyrights that the provisions of section 13 of this title have been fully complied with, and to give notice of such compliance to postmasters or to customs officers at the ports of entry in the United States in such form and accompanied by such exhibits as may be deemed necessary for the practical and efficient administration and enforcement of the provisions of sections 106 and 107 of this title.

[§ 110. See footnote 1, page 15, *supra.*]

[§ 111. See footnote 1, page 15, *supra.*]

§ 112. INJUNCTIONS; SERVICE AND ENFORCEMENT.[1]—Any court mentioned in section 1338 of Title 28 or judge thereof shall have power, upon complaint filed by any party aggrieved, to grant injunctions to prevent and restrain the violation of any right secured by this title, according to the course and principles of courts of equity, on such terms as said court or judge may deem reasonable.   Any injunction that may be granted restraining and enjoining the doing of anything forbidden by this title may be served on the parties against whom such injunction may be granted anywhere in the United States, and shall be operative throughout the United States and be enforceable by proceedings in contempt or otherwise by any other court or judge possessing jurisdiction of the defendants.

§ 113. TRANSMISSION OF CERTIFIED COPIES OF PAPERS FOR ENFORCEMENT OF INJUNCTION BY OTHER COURT.—The clerk of the court or judge granting the injunction, shall, when required so to do by the court hearing the application to enforce said injunc-

---

[1] Section 112 as amended by the Act of October 31, 1951 (65 Stat. 710, at 716, 717).

tion, transmit without delay to said court a certified copy of all the papers in said cause that are on file in his office.

§ 114. REVIEW OF ORDERS, JUDGMENTS, OR DECREES.[1]—The orders, judgments, or decrees of any court mentioned in section 1338 of Title 28 arising under the copyright laws of the United States may be reviewed on appeal in the manner and to the extent now provided by law for the review of cases determined in said courts, respectively.

§ 115. LIMITATIONS.[2]—(a) CRIMINAL PROCEEDINGS.—No criminal proceedings shall be maintained under the provisions of this title unless the same is commenced within three years after the cause of action arose.

(b) CIVIL ACTIONS.—No civil action shall be maintained under the provisions of this title unless the same is commenced within three years after the claim accrued.

§ 116. COSTS; ATTORNEY'S FEES.—In all actions, suits, or proceedings under this title, except when brought by or against the United States or any officer thereof, full costs shall be allowed, and the court may award to the prevailing party a reasonable attorney's fee as part of the costs.

CHAPTER 3—Copyright Office

§ 201. COPYRIGHT OFFICE; PRESERVATION OF RECORDS.—All rec-

[1] Section 114 as amended by the Act of October 31, 1951 (65 Stat. 710, at 716, 717).

[2] Section 115 as amended by the Act of September 7, 1957 (71 Stat. 633), effective one year after the date of enactment.

ords and other things relating to copyrights required by law to be preserved shall be kept and preserved in the copyright office, Library of Congress, District of Columbia, and shall be under the control of the register of copyrights, who shall, under the direction and supervision of the Librarian of Congress, perform all the duties relating to the registration of copyrights.

§ 202. REGISTER, ASSISTANT REGISTER, AND SUBORDINATES.— There shall be appointed by the Librarian of Congress a Register of Copyrights, and one Assistant Register of Copyrights, who shall have authority during the absence of the Register of Copyrights to attach the copyright office seal to all papers issued from the said office and to sign such certificates and other papers as may be necessary.   There shall also be appointed by the Librarian such subordinate assistants to the register as may from time to time be authorized by law.

§ 203. SAME; DEPOSIT OF MONEYS RECEIVED; REPORTS.—The Register of Copyrights shall make daily deposits in some bank in the District of Columbia, designated for this purpose by the Secretary of the Treasury as a national depository, of all moneys received to be applied as copyright fees, and shall make weekly deposits with the Secretary of the Treasury, in such manner as the latter shall direct, of all copyright fees actually applied under the provisions of this title, and annual deposits of sums received which it has not been possible to apply as copyright fees or to return to the remitters, and shall also make monthly reports to the Secretary of the Treasury and to the Librarian of Congress of the applied copyright fees for each calendar month, together with a statement of all remittances received, trust funds on hand, moneys refunded, and unapplied balances.

§ 204. SAME; BOND.—The Register of Copyrights shall give bond to the United States in the sum of $20,000, in form to be approved by the General Counsel for the Department of the Treasury and with sureties satisfactory to the Secretary of the Treasury, for the faithful discharge of his duties.

§ 205. SAME; ANNUAL REPORT.—The Register of Copyrights shall make an annual report to the Librarian of Congress, to be printed in the annual report on the Library of Congress, of all copyright business for the previous fiscal year, including the number and kind of works which have been deposited in the copyright office during the fiscal year, under the provisions of this title.

§ 206. SEAL OF COPYRIGHT OFFICE.—The seal used in the copyright office on July 1, 1909, shall be the seal of the copyright office, and by it all papers issued from the copyright office requiring authentication shall be authenticated.

§ 207. RULES FOR REGISTRATION OF CLAIMS.[1]—Subject to the approval of the Librarian of Congress, the Register of Copyrights shall be authorized to make rules and regulations for the registration of claims to copyright as provided by this title.

§ 208. RECORD BOOKS IN COPYRIGHT OFFICE.—The Register of Copyrights shall provide and keep such record books in the copyright office as are required to carry out the provisions of this title, and whenever deposit has been made in the copyright office of a copy of any work under the provisions of this title he shall make entry thereof.

§ 209. CERTIFICATE OF REGISTRATION; EFFECT AS EVIDENCE; RECEIPT FOR COPIES DEPOSITED.—In the case of each entry the person recorded as the claimant of the copyright shall be entitled to a certificate of registration under seal of the copyright office, to contain the name and address of said claimant, the name of the country of which the author of the work is a citizen or subject, and when an alien author domiciled in the United States at the time of said registration, then a statement of that fact, including his place of domicile, the name of the author (when the records of the copyright office shall show the same), the title of the work which is registered for which copyright is claimed, the date of the deposit of the copies of such work, the date of publication if the work has been reproduced in copies for sale, or publicly distributed, and such marks as to class designation and entry number as shall fully identify the entry. In the case of a book, the certificate shall also state the receipt of the affidavit, as provided by section 17 of this title, and the date of the completion of the printing, or the date of the publication of the book, as stated in the said affidavit. The Register of Copyrights shall prepare a printed form for the said certificate, to be filled out in each case as above provided for in the case of all registrations made after July 1, 1909, and in the case of all previous registrations so far as the copyright office record books shall show such facts, which certificate, sealed with the seal of the copyright office, shall, upon payment of the prescribed fee, be given to any person making application for the same. Said certificate shall be admitted in any court as prima facie evidence of the facts stated therein. In addition to such certificate the register of copyrights shall furnish, upon request, without additional fee, a receipt for the copies of the work deposited to complete the registration.

§ 210. CATALOG OF COPYRIGHT ENTRIES; EFFECT AS EVIDENCE.— The Register of Copyrights shall fully index all copyright regis-

---

[1] Published in the *Federal Register* and Title 37 of the *Code of Federal Regulations*. See Appendix, page 56, for the current regulations.

trations and assignments and shall print at periodic intervals a catalog of the titles of articles deposited and registered for copyright, together with suitable indexes, and at stated intervals shall print complete and indexed catalog for each class of copyright entries, and may thereupon, if expedient, destroy the original manuscript catalog cards containing the titles included in such printed volumes and representing the entries made during such intervals. The current catalog of copyright entries and the index volumes herein provided for shall be admitted in any court as prima facie evidence of the facts stated therein as regards any copyright registration.

§ 211. SAME; DISTRIBUTION AND SALE; DISPOSAL OF PROCEEDS.[1] —The said printed current catalogs as they are issued shall be promptly distributed by the Superintendent of Documents to the collectors of customs of the United States and to the postmasters of all exchange offices of receipt of foreign mails, in accordance with revised list of such collectors of customs and postmasters prepared by the Secretary of the Treasury and the Postmaster General, and they shall also be furnished in whole or in part to all parties desiring them at a price to be determined by the Register of Copyrights for each part of the catalog not exceeding $75 for the complete yearly catalog of copyright entries. The consolidated catalogs and indexes shall also be supplied to all persons ordering them at such prices as may be fixed by the Register of Copyrights, and all subscriptions for the catalogs shall be received by the Superintendent of Documents, who shall forward the said publications; and the moneys thus received shall be paid into the Treasury of the United States and accounted for under such laws and Treasury regulations as shall be in force at the time.

§ 212. RECORDS AND WORKS DEPOSITED IN COPYRIGHT OFFICE OPEN TO PUBLIC INSPECTION; TAKING COPIES OF ENTRIES.—The record books of the copyright office, together with the indexes to such record books, and all works deposited and retained in the copyright office, shall be open to public inspection; and copies may be taken of the copyright entries actually made in such record books, subject to such safeguards and regulations as shall be prescribed by the Register of Copyrights and approved by the Librarian of Congress.

§ 213. DISPOSITION OF ARTICLES DEPOSITED IN OFFICE.—Of the articles deposited in the copyright office under the provisions of the copyright laws of the United States, the Librarian of Congress

---

[1] Section 211 as amended by the Act of April 27, 1948 (62 Stat. 202), effective thirty days after its enactment; and the Act of October 27, 1965 (79 Stat. 1072), effective thirty days after its enactment.

shall determine what books and other articles shall be transferred to the permanent collections of the Library of Congress, including the law library, and what other books or articles shall be placed in the reserve collections of the Library of Congress for sale or exchange, or be transferred to other governmental libraries in the District of Columbia for use therein.

§ 214. DESTRUCTION OF ARTICLES DEPOSITED IN OFFICE REMAINING UNDISPOSED OF; REMOVAL OF BY AUTHOR OR PROPRIETOR; MANUSCRIPTS OF UNPUBLISHED WORKS.—Of any articles undisposed of as above provided, together with all titles and correspondence relating thereto, the Librarian of Congress and the Register of Copyrights jointly shall, at suitable intervals, determine what of these received during any period of years it is desirable or useful to preserve in the permanent files of the copyright office, and, after due notice as hereinafter provided, may within their discretion cause the remaining articles and other things to be destroyed: *Provided,* That there shall be printed in the Catalog of Copyright Entries from February to November, inclusive, a statement of the years of receipt of such articles and a notice to permit any author, copyright proprietor, or other lawful claimant to claim and remove before the expiration of the month of December of that year anything found which relates to any of his productions deposited or registered for copyright within the period of years stated, not reserved or disposed of as provided for in this title. No manuscript of an unpublished work shall be destroyed during its term of copyright without specific notice to the copyright proprietor of record, permitting him to claim and remove it.

§ 215. FEES.[1]—The Register of Copyrights shall receive, and the persons to whom the services designated are rendered shall pay, the following fees:

For the registration of a claim to copyright in any work, including a print or label used for articles of merchandise, $6; for the registration of a claim to renewal of copyright, $4; which fees shall include a certificate for each registration: *Provided,* That only one registration fee shall be required in the case of several volumes of the same book published and deposited at the same time: *And provided further,* That with respect to works of foreign origin, in lieu of payment of the copyright fee of $6 together with one copy of the work and application, the foreign author or proprietor may at any time within six months from the date of first publication abroad deposit in the Copyright Office an application for registration and two copies of the work which shall be

---

[1] Section 215 as amended by the Act of October 27, 1965 (79 Stat. 1072), effective thirty days after its enactment.

accompanied by a catalog card in form and content satisfactory to the Register of Copyrights.

For every additional certificate of registration, $2.

For certifying a copy of an application for registration of copyright, and for all other certifications, $3.

For recording every assignment, agreement, power of attorney or other paper not exceeding six pages, $5; for each additional page or less, 50 cents; for each title over one in the paper recorded, 50 cents additional.

For recording a notice of use, or notice of intention to use, $3, for each notice of not more than five titles; and 50 cents for each additional title.

For any requested search of Copyright Office records, works deposited, or other available material, or services rendered in connection therewith, $5, for each hour of time consumed.

§ 216. WHEN THE DAY FOR TAKING ACTION FALLS ON SATURDAY, SUNDAY, OR A HOLIDAY.[1]—When the last day for making any deposit or application, or for paying any fee, or for delivering any other material to the Copyright Office falls on Saturday, Sunday, or a holiday within the District of Columbia, such action may be taken on the next succeeding business day.

---

[1] Section 216 was added by the Act of April 13, 1954 (68 Stat. 52).

Schedule of Laws Repealed by Act of July 30, 1947

Section 2 of the Act of July 30, 1947 (61 Stat. 668) provides: "The following sections or parts thereof of the Revised Statutes and Statutes at Large covering provisions codified in this Act, insofar as such provisions appear in title 17, United States Code and supplements thereto, as shown by the appended table, are hereby repealed: *Provided,* That any rights or liabilities now existing under such repealed sections or parts thereof shall not be affected by such repeal:

Revised Statutes and Statutes at Large

	Title 17, United States Code, section
Act Mar. 4, 1909, ch. 320, secs. 1, 64, 35 Stat. 1075, 1088	1
Act Mar. 4, 1909, ch. 320, sec. 2, 35 Stat. 1076	2
Act Mar. 4, 1909, ch. 320, sec. 3, 35 Stat. 1076	3
Act Mar. 4, 1909, ch. 320, sec. 4, 35 Stat. 1076	4
Acts Mar. 4, 1909, ch. 320, sec. 5, 35 Stat. 1076; Aug. 24, 1912, ch. 356, 37 Stat. 488; July 31, 1939, ch. 396, sec. 2, 53 Stat. 1142	5
Act Mar. 4, 1909, ch. 320, sec. 6, 35 Stat. 1077	6
Act Mar. 4, 1909, ch. 320, secs. 7, 64, 35 Stat. 1077, 1088	7
Acts Mar. 4, 1909, ch. 320, sec. 8, 35 Stat. 1077; Dec. 18, 1919, ch. 11, 41 Stat. 369; Sept. 25, 1941, ch. 421, 55 Stat. 732	8
Act Mar. 4, 1909, ch. 320, sec. 9, 35 Stat. 1077	9
Act Mar. 4, 1909, ch. 320, sec. 10, 35 Stat. 1078	10
Acts Mar. 4, 1909, ch. 320, sec. 11, 35 Stat. 1078; Aug. 24, 1912, ch. 356, 37 Stat. 488	11
Acts Mar. 4, 1909, ch. 320, sec. 12, 35 Stat. 1078; Mar. 28, 1914, ch. 47, sec. 1, 38 Stat. 311	12
Act Mar. 4, 1909, ch. 320, sec. 13, 35 Stat. 1078	13
Act Mar. 4, 1909, ch. 320, sec. 14, 35 Stat. 1078	14
Acts Mar. 4, 1909, ch. 320, sec. 15, 35 Stat. 1078; July 3, 1926, ch. 743, 44 Stat. 818	15
Act Mar. 4, 1909, ch. 320, sec. 16, 35 Stat. 1079	16
Act Mar. 4, 1909, ch. 320, sec. 17, 35 Stat. 1079	17
Acts June 18, 1874, ch. 301, sec. 1, 18 Stat. 78; Mar. 4, 1909, ch. 320, secs. 18, 64, 35 Stat. 1079, 1088	18
Act Mar. 4, 1909, ch. 320, sec. 19, 35 Stat. 1079	19
Act Mar. 4, 1909, ch. 320, sec. 20, 35 Stat. 1080	20
Acts Mar. 4, 1909, ch. 320, sec. 21, 35 Stat. 1080; Dec. 18, 1919, ch. 11, 41 Stat. 369	21
Act Mar. 4, 1909, ch. 320, sec. 22, 35 Stat. 1080	22
Acts Mar. 4, 1909, ch. 320, sec. 23, 35 Stat. 1080; Mar. 15, 1940, ch. 57, 54 Stat. 51	23
R. S., sec. 4953; Act Mar. 4, 1909, ch. 320, secs. 24, 64, 35 Stat. 1080, 1088	24
Acts Mar. 4, 1909, ch. 320, sec. 25, 35 Stat. 1081; Aug. 24, 1912, ch. 356, 37 Stat. 489	25
Act Mar. 4, 1909, ch. 320, sec. 26, 35 Stat. 1082	26

---

[1] Corrected to "Jan. 27, 1938" by the Act of Oct. 31, 1951 (65 Stat. 710, at 716).

Parallel Reference Tables Showing Disposition of Sections of Act of March 4, 1909, as Amended, in Title 17, United States Code

Act of Mar. 4, 1909, as amended	Title 17 U. S. C.	Act of Mar. 4, 1909, as amended	Title 17 U. S. C.	Title 17 U. S. C.	Act of Mar. 4, 1909, as amended	Title 17 U. S. C.	Act of Mar. 4, 1909, as amended
1	1	33	109	1	1	¹101	25
2	2	34	¹110	2	2	¹102	26
3	3	35	¹111	3	3	¹103	27
4	4	36	112	4	4	104	28
5	5	37	113	5	5	105	29
6	7	38	114	6	(²)	106	30
7	8	39	115	7	6	107	31
8	9	40	116	8	³7	108	32
9	10	41	27	9	8	109	33
10	11	42	28	10	9	¹110	34
11	12	43	29	11	10	¹111	35
12	13	44	30	12	11	112	36
13	14	45	31	13	12	113	37
14	15	46	32	14	13	114	38
15	16	47	201	15	14	115	39
16	17	48	202	16	15	116	40
17	18	49	203	17	16	201	47
18	19	50	204	18	17	202	48
19	20	51	205	19	18	203	49
20	21	52	206	20	19	204	50
21	22	53	207	21	20	205	51
22	23	54	208	22	21	206	52
23	24	55	209	23	22	207	53
24	Omitted	56	210	24	23	208	54
25	¹101	57	211	25	(⁴)	209	55
26	¹102	58	212	26	62	210	56
27	¹103	59	213	27	41	211	57
28	104	60	214	28	42	212	58
29	105	61	215	29	43	213	59
30	106	62	26	30	44	214	60
31	107	63	Omitted	31	45	215	61
32	108	64	Omitted	32	46		

¹ Sections 101 (f), 102, 103, 110 and 111 were repealed by the Act of June 25, 1948 (62 Stat. 869).

² This was § 3 of Act of July 31, 1939 (53 Stat. 1142).

³ A portion of § 1 of Act of Jan. 27, 1938 (52 Stat. 6) is also included.

⁴ This was § 4 of the Act of July 31, 1939 (53 Stat. 1142).

APPENDIX

FOUR ACTS EXTENDING
THE DURATION OF COPYRIGHT PROTECTION
IN CERTAIN CASES

Public Law 87–668
87th Congress, H. J. Res. 627
September 19, 1962
76 STAT. 555.

Resolved by the Senate and House of Representatives of the United States of America in Congress assembled, That in any case in which the renewal term of copyright subsisting in any work on the date of approval of this resolution would expire prior to December 31, 1965, such term is hereby continued until December 31, 1965.

Approved September 19, 1962.

Public Law 89–142
89th Congress, H. J. Res. 431
August 28, 1965
79 STAT. 581.

Resolved by the Senate and House of Representatives of the United States of America in Congress assembled, That in any case in which the renewal term of copyright subsisting in any work on the date of approval of this resolution, or the term thereof as extended by Public Law 87–668, would expire prior to December 31, 1967, such term is hereby continued until December 31, 1967.

Approved August 28, 1965.

Public Law 90–141
90th Congress, S. J. Res. 114
November 16, 1967
81 STAT. 464.

Resolved by the Senate and House of Representatives of the United States of America in Congress assembled, That in any case in which the renewal term of copyright subsisting in any work on the date of approval of this resolution, or the term thereof as extended by Public Law 87–668, or by Public Law 89–142 (or by either or both of said laws), would expire prior to December 31, 1968, such term is hereby continued until December 31, 1968.

Approved November 16, 1967.

Public Law 90–416
90th Congress, S. J. Res. 172
July 23, 1968
82 STAT. 397.

Resolved by the Senate and House of Representatives of the United States of America in Congress assembled, That in any case in which the renewal term of copyright subsisting in any work on the date of approval of this resolution, or the term thereof as extended by Public Law 87–668, by Public Law 89–142, or by Public Law 90–141 (or by all or certain of said laws), would expire prior to December 31, 1969, such term is hereby continued until December 31, 1969.

Approved July 23, 1968.

Pertinent Sections of
Title 28, United States Code [1]

§ 1338. PATENTS, COPYRIGHTS, TRADE-MARKS, AND UNFAIR COMPETITION.

(a) The district courts shall have original jurisdiction of any civil action arising under any Act of Congress relating to patents, copyrights and trade-marks. Such jurisdiction shall be exclusive of the courts of the states in patent and copyright cases.

(b) The district courts shall have original jurisdiction of any civil action asserting a claim of unfair competition when joined with a substantial and related claim under the copyright, patent or trade-mark laws.

§ 1400. PATENTS AND COPYRIGHTS.

(a) Civil actions, suits, or proceedings arising under any Act of Congress relating to copyrights may be instituted in the district in which the defendant or his agent resides or may be found.

(b) Any civil action for patent infringement may be brought in the judicial district where the defendant resides, or where the defendant has committed acts of infringement and has a regular and established place of business.

§ 1498. PATENT AND COPYRIGHT CASES.

. . . .

(b) Hereafter, whenever the copyright in any work protected under the copyright laws of the United States shall be infringed by the United States, by a corporation owned or controlled by the United States, or by a contractor, subcontractor, or any person, firm, or corporation acting for the Government and with the authorization or consent of the Government, the exclusive remedy of the owner of such copyright shall be by action against the United States in the Court of Claims for the recovery of his reasonable and entire compensation as damages for such infringement, including the minimum statutory damages as set forth in section 101(b) of title 17, United States Code: *Provided,* That a

---

[1] Title 28 of the United States Code, entitled "Judiciary and Judicial Procedure" as revised, codified, and enacted into positive law by the Act of June 25, 1948 (62 Stat. 869), effective September 1, 1948. Section 1498 was amended by the Act of September 8, 1960 (74 Stat. 855). Section 2072 (page 34, *infra*) was amended by the Act of May 24, 1949 (63 Stat. 89, at 104), the Act of July 18, 1949 (63 Stat. 445), the Act of May 10, 1950 (64 Stat. 158), and the Act of July 7, 1958 (72 Stat. 339, at 348).

Government employee shall have a right of action against the Government under this subsection except where he was in a position to order, influence, or induce use of the copyrighted work by the Government: *Provided, however,* That this subsection shall not confer a right of action on any copyright owner or any assignee of such owner with respect to any copyrighted work prepared by a person while in the employment or service of the United States, where the copyrighted work was prepared as a part of the official functions of the employee, or in the preparation of which Government time, material, or facilities were used: *And provided further,* That before such action against the United States has been instituted the appropriate corporation owned or controlled by the United States or the head of the appropriate department or agency of the Government, as the case may be, is authorized to enter into an agreement with the copyright owner in full settlement and compromise for the damages accruing to him by reason of such infringement and to settle the claim administratively out of available appropriations.

Except as otherwise provided by law, no recovery shall be had for any infringement of a copyright covered by this subsection committed more than three years prior to the filing of the complaint or counter-claim for infringement in the action, except that the period between the date of receipt of a written claim for compensation by the department or agency of the Government or corporation owned or controlled by the United States, as the case may be, having authority to settle such claim and the date of mailing by the Government of a notice to the claimant that his claim has been denied shall not be counted as a part of the three years, unless suit is brought before the last-mentioned date.

(c) The provisions of this section shall not apply to any claim arising in a foreign country.

§ 2072. RULES OF CIVIL PROCEDURE FOR DISTRICT COURTS.

The Supreme Court shall have the power to prescribe, by general rules, the forms of process,[1] writs, pleadings, and motions, and the practice and procedure of the district courts of the United States in civil actions.

Such rules shall not abridge, enlarge or modify any substantive right and shall preserve the right of trial by jury as at common law and as declared by the Seventh Amendment to the Constitution.

Such rules shall not take effect until they have been reported to Congress by the Chief Justice at or after the beginning of a

---

[1] For sample form of complaint for infringement of copyright and unfair competition, see Form 17, 28 U. S. C. 6176 (appendix, 1964).

regular session thereof but not later than the first day of May, and until the expiration of ninety days after they have been thus reported.

All laws in conflict with such rules shall be of no further force or effect after such rules have taken effect. Nothing in this title, anything therein to the contrary notwithstanding, shall in any way limit, supersede, or repeal any such rules heretofore prescribed by the Supreme Court.

Rules Adopted by the Supreme Court of the United States[1] for Practice and Procedure Under Section 25[2] of an Act to Amend and Consolidate the Acts Respecting Copyright, Approved March 4, 1909

1.

Proceedings in actions brought under section 25[2] of the Act of March 4, 1909, entitled "An Act to amend and consolidate the acts respecting copyright," including proceedings relating to the perfecting of appeals, shall be governed by the Rules of Civil Procedure, insofar as they are not inconsistent with these rules.

[2.[3]]

3.

Upon the institution of any action, suit or proceeding, or at any time thereafter, and before the entry of final judgment or decree therein, the plaintiff or complainant, or his authorized agent or attorney, may file with the clerk of any court given jurisdiction under section 34[2] of the Act of March 4, 1909, an affidavit stating upon the best of his knowledge, information and belief, the number and location, as near as may be, of the alleged infringing copies, records, plates, molds, matrices, etc., or other means for making the copies alleged to infringe the copyright, and the value of the same, and with such affidavit shall file with the clerk a bond executed by at least two sureties and approved by the court or a commissioner thereof.

4.

Such bond shall bind the sureties in a specified sum, to be fixed by the court, but not less than twice the reasonable value of such

---

[1] 214 U. S. 533 (1909), as amended by 307 U. S. 652 (1939).

[2] Historical note: Sections 25 and 34 of the Act of March 4, 1909, as amended, later became sections 101 and 110, respectively, of Title 17 of the United States Code by the Act of July 30, 1947 (61 Stat. 652). Sections 101 (f) and 110 were repealed by the Act of June 25, 1948 (62 Stat. 869). However, see section 2072 of Title 28, United States Code, on page 34 of this bulletin.

[3] By amendment to the Rules of Civil Procedure for the United States District Courts, prescribed by the Supreme Court of the United States on February 28, 1966, pursuant to Title 28, U. S. C., Sec. 2072, Rule 2 was rescinded by the Court's order, effective July 1, 1966, 383 U. S. 1031.

infringing copies, plates, records, molds, matrices, or other means for making such infringing copies, and be conditioned for the prompt prosecution of the action, suit or proceeding; for the return of said articles to the defendant, if they or any of them are adjudged not to be infringements, or if the action abates, or is discontinued before they are returned to the defendant; and for the payment to the defendant of any damages which the court may award to him against the plaintiff or complainant. Upon the filing of said affidavit and bond, and the approval of said bond, the clerk shall issue a writ directed to the marshal of the district where the said infringing copies, plates, records, molds, matrices, etc., or other means of making such infringing copies shall be stated in said affidavit to be located, and generally to any marshal of the United States, directing the said marshal to forthwith seize and hold the same subject to the order of the court issuing said writ, or of the court of the district in which the seizure shall be made.

5.

The marshal shall seize said articles or any smaller or larger part thereof he may then or thereafter find, using such force as may be reasonably necessary in the premises, and serve on the defendant a copy of the affidavit, writ and bond by delivering the same to him personally, if he can be found within the district, or if he cannot be found, to his agent, if any, or to the person from whose possession the articles are taken, or if the owner, agent, or such person cannot be found within the district, by leaving said copy at the usual place of abode of such owner or agent, with a person of suitable age and discretion, or at the place where said articles are found, and shall make immediate return of such seizure, or attempted seizure, to the court. He shall also attach to said articles a tag or label stating the fact of such seizure and warning all persons from in any manner interfering therewith.

6.

A marshal who has seized alleged infringing articles, shall retain them in his possession, keeping them in a secure place, subject to the order of the court.

7.

Within three days the articles are seized, and a copy of the affidavit, writ and bond are served as hereinbefore provided, the defendant shall serve upon the clerk a notice that he excepts to the amount of the penalty of the bond, or to the sureties of the plaintiff or complainant, or both, otherwise he shall be deemed to have waived all objection to the amount of the penalty of the bond and the sufficiency of the sureties thereon. If the court sustain the exceptions it may order a new bond to be executed by the plaintiff or complainant, or in default thereof within a time to be named by the court, the property to be returned to the defendant.

8.

Within ten days after service of such notice, the attorney of the plaintiff or complainant shall serve upon the defendant or his attorney a notice of the justification of the sureties, and said sureties shall justify before the court or a judge thereof at the time therein stated.

9.

The defendant, if he does not except to the amount of the penalty of the bond or the sufficiency of the sureties of the plaintiff or complainant, may make application to the court for the return to him of the articles seized, upon filing an affidavit stating all material facts and circumstances tending to show that the articles seized are not infringing copies, records, plates, molds, matrices, or means for making the copies alleged to infringe the copyright.

10.

Thereupon the court in its discretion, after such hearing as it may direct, may order such return upon the filing by the defendant of a bond executed by at least two sureties, binding them in a specified sum to be fixed in the discretion of the court, and conditioned for the delivery of said specified articles to abide the order of the court. The plaintiff or complainant may require such sureties to justify within ten days of the filing of such bond.

11.

Upon the granting of such application and the justification of the sureties on the bond, the marshal shall immediately deliver the articles seized to the defendant.

12.

Any service required to be performed by any marshal may be performed by any deputy of such marshal.

13.

For services in cases arising under this section, the marshal shall be entitled to the same fees as are allowed for similar services in other cases.

Copyright in Territories and Insular Possessions of the United States

CANAL ZONE

Title 4, Chapter 20, Section 471 of the Canal Zone Code (approved October 18, 1962) provides:

"The patent, trade-mark, and copyright laws of the United States shall have the same force and effect in the Canal Zone as in continental United States, and the district court has the same jurisdiction in actions arising under such laws as is exercised by United States district courts."

NOTE—The Canal Zone Code is printed as a separate document, as Vol. 76A of the Statutes at Large.

GUAM

The Organic Act of Guam, § 24, 70 Stat. 908 (1956), 48 U.S.C. § 1421n (1964), provides:

"The laws of the United States relating to copyrights, and to the enforcement of rights arising thereunder, shall have the same force and effect in Guam as in the continental United States."

PUERTO RICO

The Organic Act of Puerto Rico, § 9, 39 Stat. 951 (1917), as amended, 48 U.S.C. § 734 (1964), provides in part as follows:

"That the statutory laws of the United States not locally inapplicable, except as hereinbefore or hereinafter otherwise provided, shall have the same force and effect in Puerto Rico as in the United States, * * *"

VIRGIN ISLANDS

The Organic Act of the Virgin Islands of the United States, § 18, 49 Stat. 1807 (1936), U.S.C. § 1405q (1964), provides in part as follows:

"The laws of the United States applicable to the Virgin Islands on the date of enactment of this Act, and all local laws and ordinances in force on such date in the Virgin Islands, not inconsistent with this Act, shall continue in force and effect: * * * The laws of the United States relating to patents, trade marks, and copyrights, and to the enforcement of rights arising thereunder, shall have the same force and effect in the Virgin Islands as in the continental United States, and the District Court of the Virgin Islands shall have the same jurisdiction in causes arising under such laws as is exercised by the United States district courts."

The Revised Organic Act of the Virgin Islands, § 8(c), 68 Stat. 497 (1954), 48 U.S.C. § 1574c (1964), provides in part as follows:

"The laws of the United States applicable to the Virgin Islands on the date of approval of this Act, including laws made applicable to the Virgin Islands by or pursuant to the provisions of the Act of June 22, 1936 (49 Stat. 1807), and all local laws and ordinances in force in the Virgin Islands, or any part thereof, on the date of approval of this Act, shall, to the extent they are not inconsistent with this Act, continue in force and effect until otherwise provided by the Congress: * * *"

International Copyright Relations

As of June 20, 1969, the United States has copyright relations with 69 foreign countries. Relations exist by virtue of international copyright conventions or bilateral arrangements.[1]

The Universal Copyright Convention: Effective Date; Application to Territories. The most recent convention to which the United States is a party is the Universal Copyright Convention, which came into force on September 16, 1955,[2] following ratification on November 5, 1954. It has 58 member states. This Convention is considered to be in force in the Panama Canal Zone, Puerto Rico, the Virgin Islands,[3] and Guam,[4] and in many territories or possessions of the foreign member countries. The text of the Convention, and of the three protocols thereto (which the United States also ratified), begins on page 43.

The Buenos Aires Convention. The United States is also a member of the Buenos Aires Copyright Convention of 1910,[5] to which 17 other nations of the Americas belong, most of which have also adhered to the Universal Copyright Convention.

Berne Conventions. The United States has never joined the International Union for the Protection of Literary and Artistic Works, better known as the Berne Union. At present, 59 nations are members.

Bilateral Arrangements. Some foreign states have copyright relations with the United States solely on the basis of a bilateral agreement. In certain cases, bilateral agreements also exist as to countries that have copyright relations with the United States under the Universal Copyright Convention or the Buenos Aires Convention.

The Copyright Office maintains current lists of the countries in each of the above categories, obtainable free on request from the Copyright Office, Library of Congress, Washington, D.C. 20540.

---

[1] See Appendix to TREATIES IN FORCE, published annually by the U.S. Department of State, citing proclamations, treaties and conventions establishing copyright relations.

[2] 6 U. S. T. 2731 (1955).

[3] According to letter of U.S. Ambassador Dillon in Paris to Director-General Luther Evans of Unesco, dated December 6, 1954.

[4] According to letter, dated May 14, 1957, addressed to Dr. Evans from Amory Houghton, U.S. Ambassador to France.

[5] 38 Stat. 1785 (1910).

Universal Copyright Convention [1]
Text

The Contracting States,

Moved by the desire to assure in all countries copyright protection of literary, scientific and artistic works,

Convinced that a system of copyright protection appropriate to all nations of the world and expressed in a universal convention, additional to, and without impairing international systems already in force, will ensure respect for the rights of the individual and encourage the development of literature, the sciences and the arts,

Persuaded that such a universal copyright system will facilitate a wider dissemination of works of the human mind and increase international understanding,

Have agreed as follows:

ARTICLE I

Each Contracting State undertakes to provide for the adequate and effective protection of the rights of authors and other copyright proprietors in literary, scientific and artistic works, including writings, musical, dramatic and cinematographic works, and paintings, engravings and sculpture.

ARTICLE II

1. Published works of nationals of any Contracting State and works first published in that State shall enjoy in each other Contracting State the same protection as that other State accords to works of its nationals first published in its own territory.

2. Unpublished works of nationals of each Contracting State shall enjoy in each other Contracting State the same protection as that other State accords to unpublished works of its own nationals.

3. For the purpose of this Convention any Contracting State may, by domestic legislation, assimilate to its own nationals any person domiciled in that State.

---

[1] Universal Copyright Convention (came into force September 16, 1955), 6 U. S. T. 2731 (1955).

ARTICLE III

1.   Any Contracting State which, under its domestic law, requires as a condition of copyright, compliance with formalities such as deposit, registration, notice, notarial certificates, payment of fees or manufacture or publication in that Contracting State, shall regard these requirements as satisfied with respect to all works protected in accordance with this Convention and first published outside its territory and the author of which is not one of its nationals, if from the time of the first publication all the copies of the work published with the authority of the author or other copyright proprietor bear the symbol © accompanied by the name of the copyright proprietor and the year of first publication placed in such manner and location as to give reasonable notice of claim of copyright.

2.   The provisions of paragraph 1 of this article shall not preclude any Contracting State from requiring formalities or other conditions for the acquisition and enjoyment of copyright in respect of works first published in its territory or works of its nationals wherever published.

3.   The provisions of paragraph 1 of this article shall not preclude any Contracting State from providing that a person seeking judicial relief must, in bringing the action, comply with procedural requirements, such as that the complainant must appear through domestic counsel or that the complainant must deposit with the court or an administrative office, or both, a copy of the work involved in the litigation; provided that failure to comply with such requirements shall not affect the validity of the copyright, nor shall any such requirement be imposed upon a national of another Contracting State if such requirement is not imposed on nationals of the State in which protection is claimed.

4.   In each Contracting State there shall be legal means of protecting without formalities the unpublished works of nationals of other Contracting States.

5.   If a Contracting State grants protection for more than one term of copyright and the first term is for a period longer than one of the minimum periods prescribed in article IV, such State shall not be required to comply with the provisions of paragraph 1 of this article III in respect of the second or any subsequent term of copyright.

ARTICLE IV

1.   The duration of protection of a work shall be governed, in accordance with the provisions of article II and this article, by

the law of the Contracting State in which protection is claimed.

2. The term of protection for works protected under this Convention shall not be less than the life of the author and 25 years after his death.

However, any Contracting State which, on the effective date of this Convention in that State, has limited this term for certain classes of works to a period computed from the first publication of the work, shall be entitled to maintain these exceptions and to extend them to other classes of works. For all these classes the term of protection shall not be less than 25 years from the date of first publication.

Any Contracting State which, upon the effective date of this Convention in that State, does not compute the term of protection upon the basis of the life of the author, shall be entitled to compute the term of protection from the date of the first publication of the work or from its registration prior to publication, as the case may be, provided the term of protection shall not be less than 25 years from the date of first publication or from its registration prior to publication, as the case may be.

If the legislation of a Contracting State grants two or more successive terms of protection, the duration of the first term shall not be less than one of the minimum periods specified above.

3. The provisions of paragraph 2 of this article shall not apply to photographic works or to works of applied art; provided, however, that the term of protection in those Contracting States which protect photographic works, or works of applied art in so far as they are protected as artistic works, shall not be less than ten years for each of said classes of works.

4. No Contracting State shall be obliged to grant protection to a work for a period longer than that fixed for the class of works to which the work in question belongs, in the case of unpublished works by the law of the Contracting State of which the author is a national, and in the case of published works by the law of the Contracting State in which the work has been first published.

For the purposes of the application of the preceding provision, if the law of any Contracting State grants two or more successive terms of protection, the period of protection of that State shall be considered to be the aggregate of those terms. However, if a specified work is not protected by such State during the second or any subsequent term for any reason, the other Contracting States shall not be obliged to protect it during the second or any subsequent term.

5. For the purposes of the application of paragraph 4 of this article, the work of a national of a Contracting State, first pub-

lished in a non-Contracting State, shall be treated as though first published in the Contracting State of which the author is a national.

6. For the purposes of the application of paragraph 4 of this article, in case of simultaneous publication in two or more Contracting States, the work shall be treated as though first published in the State which affords the shortest term; any work published in two or more Contracting States within thirty days of its first publication shall be considered as having been published simultaneously in said Contracting States.

ARTICLE V

1. Copyright shall include the exclusive right of the author to make, publish, and authorize the making and publication of translations of works protected under this Convention.

2. However, any Contracting State may, by its domestic legislation, restrict the right of translation of writings, but only subject to the following provisions:

If, after the expiration of a period of seven years from the date of the first publication of a writing, a translation of such writing has not been published in the national language or languages, as the case may be, of the Contracting State, by the owner of the right of translation or with his authorization, any national of such Contracting State may obtain a non-exclusive license from the competent authority thereof to translate the work and publish the work so translated in any of the national languages in which it has not been published; provided that such national, in accordance with the procedure of the State concerned, establishes either that he has requested, and been denied, authorization by the proprietor of the right to make and publish the translation, or that, after due diligence on his part, he was unable to find the owner of the right. A license may also be granted on the same conditions if all previous editions of a translation in such language are out of print.

If the owner of the right of translation cannot be found, then the applicant for a license shall send copies of his application to the publisher whose name appears on the work and, if the nationality of the owner of the right of translation is known, to the diplomatic or consular representative of the State of which such owner is a national, or to the organization which may have been designated by the government of that State. The license shall not be granted before the expiration of a period of two months from the date of the dispatch of the copies of the application.

Due provision shall be made by domestic legislation to assure to the owner of the right of translation a compensation which is just and conforms to international standards, to assure payment and transmittal of such compensation, and to assure a correct translation of the work.

The original title and the name of the author of the work shall be printed on all copies of the published translation. The license shall be valid only for publication of the translation in the territory of the Contracting State where it has been applied for. Copies so published may be imported and sold in another Contracting State if one of the national languages of such other State is the same language as that into which the work has been so translated, and if the domestic law in such other State makes provision for such licences and does not prohibit such importation and sale. Where the foregoing conditions do not exist, the importation and sale of such copies in a Contracting State shall be governed by its domestic law and its agreements. The licence shall not be transferred by the license.

The license shall not be granted when the author has withdrawn from circulation all copies of the work.

ARTICLE VI

"Publication," as used in this Convention, means the reproduction in tangible form and the general distribution to the public of copies of a work from which it can be read or otherwise visually perceived.

ARTICLE VII

This Convention shall not apply to works or rights in works which, at the effective date of the Convention in a Contracting State where protection is claimed, are permanently in the public domain in the said Contracting State.

ARTICLE VIII

1. This Convention, which shall bear the date of September 6 1952, shall be deposited with the Director-General of the United Nations Educational, Scientific and Cultural Organization and shall remain open for signature by all States for a period of 120 days after that date. It shall be subject to ratification or acceptance by the signatory States.

2. Any State which has not signed this Convention may accede thereto.

3. Ratification, acceptance or accession shall be effected by the deposit of an instrument to that effect with the Director-General

of the United Nations Educational, Scientific and Cultural
Organization.

ARTICLE IX

1.   This Convention shall come into force three months after
the deposit of twelve instruments of ratification, acceptance or
accession, among which there shall be those of four States which
are not members of the International Union for the Protection
of Literary and Artistic Works.

2.   Subsequently, this Convention shall come into force in
respect of each State three months after that State has deposited
its instrument of ratification, acceptance or accession.

ARTICLE X

1.   Each State party to this Convention undertakes to adopt,
in accordance with its Constitution, such measures as are necessary to ensure the application of this Convention.

2.   It is understood, however, that at the time an instrument
of ratification, acceptance or accession is deposited on behalf of
any State, such State must be in a position under its domestic law
to give effect to the terms of this Convention.

ARTICLE XI

1.   An Intergovernmental Committee is hereby established with
the following duties:

   (a) to study the problems concerning the application and
       operation of this Convention;
   (b) to make preparation for periodic revisions of this Con-
       vention;
   (c) to study any other problems concerning the international
       protection of copyright, in co-operation with the various
       interested international organizations, such as the United
       Nations Educational, Scientific and Cultural Organization,
       the International Union for the Protection of Literary and
       Artistic Works and the Organization of American States;
   (d) to inform the Contracting States as to its activities.

2.   The Committee shall consist of the representatives of
twelve Contracting States to be selected with due consideration to
fair geographical representation and in conformity with the Resolution relating to this article, annexed to this Convention.

The Director-General of the United Nations Educational, Scientific and Cultural Organization, the Director of the Bureau of the

International Union for the Protection of Literary and Artistic Works and the Secretary-General of the Organization of American States, or their representatives, may attend meetings of the Committee in an advisory capacity.

ARTICLE XII

The Intergovernmental Committee shall convene a conference for revision of this Convention whenever it deems necessary, or at the request of at least ten Contracting States, or of a majority of the Contracting States if there are less than twenty Contracting States.

ARTICLE XIII

Any Contracting State may, at the time of deposit of its instrument of ratification, acceptance or accession, or at any time thereafter, declare by notification addressed to the Director-General of the United Nations Educational, Scientific and Cultural Organization that this Convention shall apply to all or any of the countries or territories for the international relations of which it is responsible and this Convention shall thereupon apply to the countries or territories named in such notification after the expiration of the term of three months provided for in article IX. In the absence of such notification, this Convention shall not apply to any such country or territory.

ARTICLE XIV

1.   Any Contracting State may denounce this Convention in its own name or on behalf of all or any of the countries or territories as to which a notification has been given under article XIII. The denunciation shall be made by notification addressed to the Director-General of the United Nations Educational, Scientific and Cultural Organization.

2.   Such denunciation shall operate only in respect of the State or of the country or territory on whose behalf it was made and shall not take effect until twelve months after the date of receipt of the notification.

ARTICLE XV

A dispute between two or more Contracting States concerning the interpretation or application of this Convention, not settled by negotiation, shall, unless the States concerned agree on some other method of settlement, be brought before the International Court of Justice for determination by it.

ARTICLE XVI

1. This Convention shall be established in English, French and Spanish. The three texts shall be signed and shall be equally authoritative.

2. Official texts of this Convention shall be established in German, Italian and Portuguese.

Any Contracting State or group of Contracting States shall be entitled to have established by the Director-General of the United Nations Educational, Scientific and Cultural Organization other texts in the language of its choice by arrangement with the Director-General.

All such texts shall be annexed to the signed texts of this Convention.

ARTICLE XVII

1. This Convention shall not in any way affect the provisions of the Berne Convention for the Protection of Literary and Artistic Works or membership in the Union created by that Convention.

2. In application of the foregoing paragraph, a Declaration has been annexed to the present article. This Declaration is an integral part of this Convention for the States bound by the Berne Convention on January 1, 1951, or which have or may become bound to it at a later date. The signature of this Convention by such States shall also constitute signature of the said Declaration, and ratification, acceptance or accession by such States shall include the Declaration as well as the Convention.

ARTICLE XVIII

This Convention shall not abrogate multilateral or bilateral copyright conventions or arrangements that are or may be in effect exclusively between two or more American Republics. In the event of any difference either between the provisions of such existing conventions or arrangements and the provisions of this Convention, or between the provisions of this Convention and those of any new convention or arrangement which may be formulated between two or more American Republics after this Convention comes into force, the convention or arrangement most recently formulated shall prevail between the parties thereto. Rights in works acquired in any Contracting State under existing conventions or arrangements before the date this Convention comes into force in such State shall not be affected.

ARTICLE XIX

This Convention shall not abrogate multilateral or bilateral conventions or arrangements in effect between two or more Contracting States.   In the event of any difference between the provisions of such existing conventions or arrangements and the provisions of this Convention, the provisions of this Convention shall prevail.   Rights in works acquired in any Contracting State under existing conventions or arrangements before the date on which this Convention comes into force in such State shall not be affected.   Nothing in this article shall affect the provisions of articles XVII and XVIII of this Convention.

ARTICLE XX

Reservations to this Convention shall not be permitted.

ARTICLE XXI

The Director-General of the United Nations Educational, Scientific and Cultural Organization shall send duly certified copies of this Convention to the States interested, to the Swiss Federal Council and to the Secretary-General of the United Nations for registration by him.

He shall also inform all interested States of the ratifications, acceptances and accessions which have been deposited, the date on which this Convention comes into force, the notifications under Article XIII of this Convention, and denunciations under Article XIV.

APPENDIX DECLARATION
relating to Article XVII

The States which are members of the International Union for the Protection of Literary and Artistic Works, and which are signatories to the Universal Copyright Convention,

Desiring to reinforce their mutual relations on the basis of the said Union and to avoid any conflict which might result from the co-existence of the Convention of Berne and the Universal Convention,

Have, by common agreement, accepted the terms of the following declaration:

(a) Works which, according to the Berne Convention, have as their country of origin a country which has withdrawn from the International Union created by the said Convention, after January 1, 1951, shall not be protected by the

Universal Copyright Convention in the countries of the Berne Union;

(b) The Universal Copyright Convention shall not be applicable to the relationships among countries of the Berne Union insofar as it relates to the protection of works having as their country of origin, within the meaning of the Berne Convention, a country of the International Union created by the said Convention.

RESOLUTION CONCERNING
ARTICLE XI
The Intergovernmental Copyright Conference

Having considered the problems relating to the Intergovernmental Committee provided for in Article XI of the Universal Copyright Convention

resolves

1. The first members of the Committee shall be representatives of the following twelve States, each of those States designating one representative and an alternate: Argentine, Brazil, France, Germany, India, Italy, Japan, Mexico, Spain, Switzerland, United Kingdom, and United States of America.

2. The Committee shall be constituted as soon as the Convention comes into force in accordance with article XI of this Convention;

3. The Committee shall elect its Chairman and one Vice-Chairman. It shall establish its rules of procedure having regard to the following principles:

(a) the normal duration of the term of office of the representatives shall be six years; with one third retiring every two years;

(b) before the expiration of the term of office of any members, the Committee shall decide which States shall cease to be represented on it and which States shall be called upon to designate representatives; the representatives of those States which have not ratified, accepted or acceded shall be the first to retire;

(c) the different parts of the world shall be fairly represented;

and expresses the wish

that the United Nations Educational, Scientific, and Cultural Organization provide its Secretariat.

In faith whereof the undersigned, having deposited their respective full powers, have signed this Convention.

Done at Geneva, this sixth day of September, 1952 in a single copy.

Protocol 1 to the Universal Copyright Convention concerning the application of that Convention to the works of stateless persons and refugees

The States parties hereto, being also parties to the Universal Copyright Convention (hereinafter referred to as the "Convention") have accepted the following provisions:

1. Stateless persons and refugees who have their habitual residence in a State party to this Protocol shall, for the purposes of the Convention, be assimilated to the nationals of that State.

2. (a) This Protocol shall be signed and shall be subject to ratification or acceptance, or may be acceded to, as if the provisions of article VIII of the Convention applied hereto.

(b) This Protocol shall enter into force in respect of each State, on the date of deposit of the instrument of ratification, acceptance or accession of the State concerned or on the date of entry into force of the Convention with respect to such State, whichever is the later.

In faith whereof the undersigned, being duly authorised thereto, have signed this Protocol.

Done at Geneva this sixth day of September, 1952, in the English, French and Spanish languages, the three texts being equally authoritative, in a single copy which shall be deposited with the Director-General of Unesco. The Director-General shall send certified copies to the signatory States, to the Swiss Federal Council and to the Secretary-General of the United Nations for registration.

Protocol 2 annexed to the Universal Copyright Convention, concerning the application of that Convention to the works of certain international organisations

The State parties hereto, being also parties to the Universal Copyright Convention (hereinafter referred to as the "Convention"),

Have accepted the following provisions:

1. (a) The protection provided for in article II (1) of the Convention shall apply to works published for the first time by the United Nations, by the Specialized Agencies in relationship therewith, or by the Organisation of American States;

(b) Similarly, article II (2) of the Convention shall apply to the said organisation or agencies.

2. (a) This Protocol shall be signed and shall be subject to

ratification or acceptance, or may be acceded to, as if the provisions of article VIII of the Convention applied hereto.

(b) This Protocol shall enter into force for each State on the date of deposit of the instrument of ratification, acceptance or accession of the State concerned or on the date of entry into force of the Convention with respect to such State, whichever is the later.

In faith whereof the undersigned, being duly authorised thereto, have signed this Protocol.

Done at Geneva, this sixth day of September, 1952, in the English, French and Spanish languages, the three texts being equally authoritative, in a single copy which shall be deposited with the Director-General of the Unesco.

The Director-General shall send certificated copies to the signatory States, to the Swiss Federal Council, and to the Secretary-General of the United Nations for registration.

Protocol 3 annexed to the Universal Copyright Convention concerning the effective date of instruments of ratification or acceptance of or accession to that Convention

States parties hereto,

Recognizing that the application of the Universal Copyright Convention (hereinafter referred to as the "Convention") to States participating in all the international copyright systems already in force will contribute greatly to the value of the Convention;

Have agreed as follows:

1. Any State party hereto may, on depositing its instrument of ratification or acceptance of or accession to the Convention, notify the Director-General of the United Nations Educational, Scientific and Cultural Organization (hereinafter referred to as "Director-General") that that instrument shall not take effect for the purposes of Article IX of the Convention until any other State named in such notification shall have deposited its instrument.

2. The notification referred to in paragraph 1 above shall accompany the instrument to which it relates.

3. The Director-General shall inform all States signatory or which have then acceded to the Convention of any notifications received in accordance with this Protocol.

4. This Protocol shall bear the same date and shall remain open for signature for the same period as the Convention.

5. It shall be subject to ratification or acceptance by the

signatory States. Any State which has not signed this Protocol may accede thereto.

6. (a) Ratification or acceptance or accession shall be effected by the deposit of an instrument to that effect with the Director-General.

(b) This Protocol shall enter into force on the date of deposit of not less than four instruments of ratification or acceptance or accession. The Director-General shall inform all interested States of this date. Instruments deposited after such date shall take effect on the date of their deposit.

In faith whereof the undersigned, being duly authorised thereto, have signed this Protocol.

Done at Geneva, the sixth day of September 1952, in the English, French and the Spanish languages, the three texts being equally authoritative, in a single copy which shall be annexed to the original copy of the Convention. The Director-General shall send certified copies to the signatory States, to the Swiss Federal Council, and to the Secretary-General of the United Nations for registration.

Regulations of the Copyright Office [1]

(As amended through July 4, 1967)

PART 201—GENERAL PROVISIONS

AUTHORITY: §§ 201.1 to 201.8 issued under sec. 207, 61 Stat. 666; 17 U.S.C. § 207.

§201.1 COMMUNICATIONS WITH THE COPYRIGHT OFFICE.

Mail and other communications shall be addressed to the Register of Copyrights, Library of Congress, Washington, D.C. 20540.

§ 201.2 INFORMATION GIVEN BY THE COPYRIGHT OFFICE.

(a) *In general.* (1) Information relative to the operations of the Copyright Office is supplied without charge. A search of the records, indexes and deposits will be made for such information as they may contain relative to copyright claims upon application and payment of the statutory fee. The Copyright Office, however, does not undertake the making of comparisons of copyright deposits to determine similarity between works, nor does it give legal opinions or advice on such matters as:

(i) The validity or status of any copyright other than the facts shown in the records of the Office;

(ii) The rights of persons, whether in connection with cases of alleged copyright infringement, contracts between authors and publishers or other matters of a similar nature;

(iii) The scope and extent of protection of works in foreign countries or interpretation of foreign copyright laws or court opinions;

(iv) The sufficiency, extent or scope of compliance with the copyright law.

---

[1] *Code of Federal Regulations,* Title 37, Chapter II (*Federal Register,* volume 24, page 4955, June 18, 1959). Section 201.3 as amended, *Federal Register,* volume 31, page 6119, April 21, 1966. Section 201.2 as amended, *Federal Register,* volume 32, pages 9314–9315, June 30, 1967, effective July 4, 1967.

(2) In addition, the Office cannot undertake to furnish the names of copyright attorneys, publishers, agents, or other similar information.

(b) *Inspection and copying of records.* (1) Inspection and copying of completed records and indexes relating to a registration or a recorded document, and inspection of copies deposited in connection with a completed copyright registration, may be undertaken at such times as will not result in interference with or delay in the work of the Copyright Office.

(2) The copying from the Copyright Office records of names and addresses for the purpose of compiling mailing lists and other similar uses is expressly prohibited.

(3) The Copyright Office maintains an administrative staff manual, referred to as its "Compendium of Office Practices," and an index to the manual, for the general guidance of its staff in making registrations and recording documents. The manual and index, as amended and supplemented from time to time, are available in the Copyright Office for public inspection and copying.

(c) *Correspondence.* (1) Official correspondence, including preliminary applications, between copyright claimants or their agents and the Copyright Office, and directly relating to a completed registration or to a recorded document, is made available for public inspection. Requests for photocopies of the correspondence shall be made pursuant to paragraph (d) of this section.

(2) (i) Correspondence, application forms and any accompanying material forming a part of a pending or rejected application are not records which are open to public inspection under paragraph (b) of this section.

(ii) Inspection of such files may be afforded upon presentation of written authorization of the claimant or his agent, or upon submission to the Register of Copyrights, Library of Congress, Washington, D.C. 20540, of a written request which is deemed by him to show good cause for such access and which establishes that the person making the request is one properly and directly concerned.

(iii) Where such access is authorized and photocopies of the official file are subsequently requested, the conditions and procedures of paragraph (d) of this section are controlling.

(3) Correspondence, memoranda, reports, opinions, and similar material relating to internal matters of personnel and procedures, office administration, security matters, and internal consideration of policy and decisional matters, including the work product of an attorney, are not open to public inspection.

(4) The Copyright Office will return unanswered any abusive or scurrilous correspondence.

(d) *Requests for copies.* (1) Requests for additional certificates of registration should be sent to the Copyright Office, and the accompanying fees should be made payable to the Register of Copyrights.

(2) Requests for photocopies of copyright deposits, official correspondence, and Copyright Office records (other than additional certificates of registration) should be sent to the Chief, Photoduplication Service, Library of Congress, Washington, D.C. 20540, the accompanying fees in payment of such services being made payable to that official. When the photocopy is to be certified by the Copyright Office, the additional certification fee should be made payable to the Register of Copyrights and both remittances together with the transmittal letter are to be sent to the Copyright Office.

(3) Requests for photocopies of official correspondence shall identify the specific material desired and shall contain a statement enabling the Copyright Office to determine if the writer is properly and directly concerned.

(4) Requests for photocopies of copyright deposits will be granted when one or more of the following conditions are fulfilled:

(i) *Authorization by owner.* When authorized in writing by the copyright owner or his designated agent.

(ii) *Request by attorney.* When required in connection with litigation, actual or prospective, in which the copyrighted work is involved; but in all such cases the attorney representing the actual or prospective plaintiff or defendant for whom the request is made shall give in writing: (a) The names of the parties and the nature of the controversy; (b) the name of the court where the action is pending, or, in the case of a prospective proceeding, a full statement of the facts of the controversy in which the copyrighted work is involved; and (c) satisfactory assurances that the requested copy will be used only in connection with the specified litigation.

(iii) *Court order.* When an order to have the copy made is issued by a court having jurisdiction of a case in which the copy is to be submitted as evidence.

§ 201.3 CATALOG OF COPYRIGHT ENTRIES.

The subscription price for all parts of the complete yearly Catalog of Copyright Entries, effective with Volume 20, is $50.00. Each part of the Catalog is published in two semiannual numbers covering, respectively, the periods January–June and July–December. The prices given in the list below are for each semiannual number; the price of an annual subscription to any part is twice the price of the semiannual number. The entire annual Catalog or any of its parts may be obtained, upon payment of the established price, from the Superintendent of Documents, Government Printing Office, Washington, D.C. 20402, to whom requests for copies should be addressed and to whom the remittance should be made payable.

Part 1—Books and Pamphlets Including Serials and Contributions to Periodicals, $7.50.

Part 2—Periodicals, $2.50.

Parts 3–4—Dramas and Works Prepared for Oral Delivery, $2.50.

Part 5—Music, $7.50.

Part 6—Maps and Atlases, $2.50.

Parts 7–11A—Works of Art, Reproductions of Works of Art, Scientific and Technical Drawings, Photographic Works, Prints and Pictorial Illustrations, $2.50.

Part 11B—Commercial Prints and Labels, $2.50.

Parts 12–13—Motion Pictures and Filmstrips, $2.50.

§ 201.4 ASSIGNMENTS OF COPYRIGHT AND OTHER PAPERS.

Assignments of copyright and other papers relative to copyrights will be recorded in the Copyright Office upon payment of the statutory fee. Examples of such papers include powers of attorney, licenses to use a copyrighted work, agreements between authors and publishers covering a particular work or works and the rights thereto, mortgages, certificates of change of corporate title, wills, and decrees of distribution. The original, signed instrument should be submitted for recordation, and is returned to the sender with a certificate of record. Where the original instrument is not available, a certified or other copy may be submitted, but it shall be accompanied by a statement that the original is not available.

§ 201.5 AMENDMENTS TO COMPLETED COPYRIGHT OFFICE REGISTRATIONS AND OTHER RECORDS.

(a) *No cancellations.* No correction or cancellation of a Copyright Office registration or other record will be made (other than a registration or record provisional upon receipt of fee as provided in § 201.6) after it has been completed if the facts therein stated agree with those supplied the Office for the purpose of making such record. However, it shall be within the discretion of the Register of Copyrights to determine if any particular case justifies the placing of an annotation upon any record for the purpose of clarification, explanation, or indication that there exists elsewhere in the records, indexes or correspondence files of the Office, information which has reference to the facts as stated in such record.

(b) *Correction by new registration.* In exceptional cases, where an applicant desires to correct, amend or amplify a registration previously made in accordance with information furnished by a claimant or his agent, a new application indicating its amendatory purpose shall be filed, accompanied by the statutory fee and the same number of copies required for a new application. Where it is satisfactorily established that copies of the original work cannot be obtained for submission, photocopies or microfilm copies of the original may be submitted.

§ 201.6 PAYMENT AND REFUND OF COPYRIGHT OFFICE FEES.

(a) *In general.* All fees sent to the Copyright Office should be in the form of a money order, check or bank draft payable to the Register of Copyrights. Coin or currency sent to the Office in letters or packages will be at the remitter's risk. Remittances from foreign countries should be in the form of an International Money Order or Bank Draft payable and immediately negotiable in the United States for the full amount of the fee required. Uncertified checks are accepted subject to collection. Where the statutory fee is submitted in the form of a check, the registration of the copyright claim or other record made by the Office is provisional until payment in money is received. In the event the fee is not paid, the registration or other record shall be expunged.

(b) *Deposit accounts.* Persons or firms having a considerable amount of business with the Copyright Office may, for their own convenience, prepay copyright expenses by establishing a Deposit Account.

(c) *Refunds.* Money paid for applications which are rejected or payments made in excess of the statutory fee will be refunded, but amounts of twenty-five cents or less will not be returned unless specifically requested and such sums may be refunded in postage stamps. All larger amounts will be refunded by check.

(d) *Return of deposit copies.* Copies of works deposited in the Copyright Office pursuant to law are either retained in the Copyright Office, transferred for the permanent collections or other uses of the Library of Congress, or disposed of according to law. When an application is rejected, the Copyright Office reserves the right to retain the deposited copies.

§ 201.7 PREPARATION OF CATALOG CARD.

The catalog card which may accompany a work of foreign origin, as provided in section 215 of title 17, U.S. Code, as amended, may be a catalog card supplied by a library in the country of publication. In lieu of such a card the applicant may prepare his own card, or may fill out the form supplied by the Copyright Office. The catalog card should contain the full name of the author of the original work, title and description from the title page, paging, copyright claimant, the city and year of publication, and the names of all other authors, editors, etc., whom the applicant considers of sufficient importance to record. When available, the year of birth of each author named should be given. If the form furnished by the Office is not used, the size of the card should preferably be 5 inches wide by 3 inches deep or 12.5 centimeters wide by 7.5 centimeters deep. The Register of Copyrights reserves the right to accept catalog cards not complying with the above requirements.

§ 201.8 IMPORT STATEMENTS.

(a) The Copyright Office will issue import statements for books and periodicals first published abroad in the English language which are to be imported under the provisions of section 16 of title 17, U.S. Code, as amended. A statement for the importation of 1,500 copies will be issued to the person named in the application for ad interim copyright registration. The holder of this statement shall present it to the customs officer in charge of the port of entry. Upon receipt of a statement from the customs officer, showing importation of less than 1,500 copies, a new statement will be issued for the balance.

(b) The provisions in the Customs Regulations covering the use of the import statement (Copyright Office Form C–100) are found in 19 CFR 11.21 (21 F.R. 2517).

PART 202—REGISTRATION OF CLAIMS TO COPYRIGHT

202.9   Maps (Class F).
202.10   Works of art (Class G).
202.11   Reproductions of works of art (Class H).
202.12   Drawings or plastic works of a scientific or technical character (Class I).
202.13   Photographs (Class J).
202.14   Prints, pictorial illustrations and commercial prints or labels (Class K).
202.15   Motion pictures (Classes L–M).
202.16   Deposit of photographs or other identifying reproductions in lieu of copies.
202.17   Renewals.
202.18   Notices of use.

AUTHORITY: §§ 202.1 to 202.18 issued under sec. 207, 61 Stat. 666; 17 U.S.C. § 207.

§ 202.1   MATERIAL NOT SUBJECT TO COPYRIGHT.

The following are examples of works not subject to copyright and applications for registration of such works cannot be entertained:

(a) Words and short phrases such as names, titles, and slogans; familiar symbols or designs; mere variations of typographic ornamentation, lettering or coloring; mere listing of ingredients or contents;

(b) Ideas, plans, methods, systems, or devices, as distinguished from the particular manner in which they are expressed or described in a writing;

(c) Works designed for recording information which do not in themselves convey information, such as time cards, graph paper, account books, diaries, bank checks, score cards, address books, report forms, order forms and the like;

(d) Works consisting entirely of information that is common property containing no original authorship, such as, for example: Standard calendars, height and weight charts, tape measures and rulers, schedules of sporting events, and lists or tables taken from public documents or other common sources.

§ 202.2   COPYRIGHT NOTICE.

(a) *General.*   (1) With respect to a published work, copyright is secured, or the right to secure it is lost, at the date of publication, i.e., the date on which copies are first placed on sale, sold, or publicly distributed, depending upon the adequacy of the notice of copyright on the work at that time.

(2) If publication occurs by distribution of copies or in some other manner, without the statutory notice or with an inadequate

notice, the right to secure copyright is lost. In such cases, copyright cannot be secured by adding the notice to copies distributed at a later date.

(3) Works first published abroad, other than works eligible for ad interim registration, must bear an adequate copyright notice at the time of their first publication in order to secure copyright under the law of the United States.

(b) *Defects in notice.* Where the copyright notice does not meet the requirements of the law, the Copyright Office will reject an application for copyright registration. Common defects in the notice include, among others, the following:

(1) The notice lacks one or more of the necessary elements (i.e., the word "Copyright," the abbreviation "Copr.," or the symbol ©; the name of the copyright proprietor; or, when required, the year date of publication);

(2) The elements of the notice are dispersed;

(3) The notice is not in one of the positions prescribed by law;

(4) The notice is in a foreign language;

(5) The name in the notice is that of someone who had no authority to secure copyright in his name;

(6) The year date in the copyright notice is later than the date of the year in which copyright was actually secured, including the following cases:

(i) Where the year date in the notice is later than the date of actual publication;

(ii) Where copyright was first secured by registration of a work in unpublished form, and copies of the same work as later published without change in substance bear a copyright notice containing a year date later than the year of unpublished registration;

(iii) Where a book or periodical published abroad, for which ad interim copyright has been obtained, is later published in the United States without change in substance and contains a year date in the copyright notice later than the year of first publication abroad: *Provided, however,* That in each of the three foregoing types of cases, if the copyright was actually secured not more than one year earlier than the year date in the notice, registration may be considered as a doubtful case.

(7) A notice is permanently covered so that it cannot be seen without tearing the work apart;

(8) A notice is illegible or so small that it cannot be read without the aid of a magnifying glass: *Provided, however,* That where the work itself requires magnification for its ordinary use (e.g.,

a microfilm, microcard or motion picture) a notice which will be readable when so magnified, will not constitute a reason for rejection of the claim;

(9) A notice is on a detachable tag and will eventually be detached and discarded when the work is put in use;

(10) A notice is on the wrapper or container which is not a part of the work and which will eventually be removed and discarded when the work is put in use;

(11) The notice is restricted or limited exclusively to an uncopyrightable element, either by virtue of its position on the work, by the use of asterisks, or by other means.

§ 202.3 APPLICATION FORMS.

(a) *In general.*   Section 5 of title 17 of the U.S. Code provides thirteen classes (Class A through Class M) of works in which copyright may be claimed.   Examples of certain works falling within these classes are given in §§ 202.4 to 202.15 inclusive, for the purpose of assisting persons who desire to obtain registration of a claim to copyright, to select the correct application form.

(b) *Claims of copyright.*   (1) All works deposited for registration shall be accompanied by a "claim of copyright" in the form of a properly executed application, together with the statutory registration fee.   The Office reserves the right to refuse to accept any application that is a carbon copy, illegible, defaced, or otherwise not in an acceptable condition for examination and recording.

(2) Where these separate elements are not received simultaneously, the Copyright Office holds the submitted elements for a reasonable time and, in default of the receipt of the missing element or elements after a request made therefor, the submitted item or items may be returned to the sender.   Such action does not constitute a waiver of the right of the Register of Copyrights pursuant to section 14, title 17, U.S. Code, to demand compliance with the deposit provisions of that title.

(3) Applications for copyright registration covering published works should reflect the facts existing at the time of first publication, and should not include information concerning changes that have occurred between the time of publication and registration. The name given as copyright claimant in the application should agree with the name appearing in the copyright notice.

(4) Applications should be submitted by the copyright claimant, or by someone acting under his authority.

(5) All information requested by the Copyright Office application form should be given in the appropriate spaces provided. There should not be attached to the application any slips of paper

or extra pages containing additional information, or a continuation of requested information.

(c) *Forms.* The Copyright Office supplies without charge the following forms for use when applying for the registration of a claim to copyright in a work and for the filing of a notice of use of musical compositions on mechanical instruments.

Form A—Published book manufactured in the United States of America (Class A).

Form A–B Ad Interim—Book or periodical in the English language manufactured and first published outside the United States of America (Classes A–B).

Form A–B Foreign—Book or periodical manufactured outside the United States of America (except works subject to the ad interim provisions of the copyright law) (Classes A–B).

Form B—Periodical manufactured in the United States of America (Class B).

Form BB—Contribution to a periodical manufactured in the United States of America (Class B).

Form C—Lecture or similar production prepared for oral delivery (Class C).

Form D—Dramatic or dramatico-musical composition (Class D).

Form E—Musical composition the author of which is a citizen or domiciliary of the United States of America or which was published in the United States of America (Class E).

Form E Foreign—Musical composition the author of which is not a citizen or domiciliary of the United States of America and which was not first published in the United States of America (Class E).

Form F—Map (Class F).

Form G—Work of art or a model or design for a work of art (Class G).

Form H—Reproduction of a work of art (Class H).

Form I—Drawing or plastic work of a scientific or technical character (Class I).

Form J—Photograph (Class J).

Form K—Print or pictorial illustration (Class K).

Form KK—Print or label used for an article of merchandise (Class K).

Form L–M—Motion picture (Classes L–M).

Form R—Renewal copyright.

Form U—Notice of use of copyrighted music on mechanical instruments.

§ 202.4 BOOKS (CLASS A).

(a) *Subject matter and forms.* This class includes such published works as fiction and nonfiction, poems, compilations, composite works, directories, catalogs, annual publications, information in tabular form, and similar text matter, with or without illustrations, as books, either bound or in loose-leaf form, pamphlets, leaflets, cards, single pages or the like. Applications for registration of claims to copyright in published books manufactured in the United States of America are made on Form A; in books manufactured outside of the United States of America, except those subject to ad interim provisions of the copyright law, on Form A–B Foreign; and in books in the English language manufactured and first published outside the United States of America, and subject to the ad interim provisions of the copyright law, on Form A–B Ad Interim.

(b) *Ad interim registrations.* (1) An American edition of an English-language book or periodical identical in substance to that first published abroad will not be registered unless an ad interim registration is first made.

(2) When a book or periodical has been registered under the ad interim provisions, an American edition of the same work, to be registrable, must be manufactured and published in the United States within five years after the date of first publication abroad.

(3) Since by law ad interim copyright expires at the end of the ad interim term unless an American edition is published during that term, a renewal application covering a work registered only under the ad interim provisions will be rejected. Where both an ad interim and an American edition have been registered, the registrability of the renewal application is governed by the date of the first publication abroad.

§ 202.5 PERIODICALS (CLASS B).

This class includes such works as newspapers, magazines, reviews, bulletins, and serial publications, published at intervals of less than a year. Applications for registration of claims to copyright in published periodicals manufactured in the United States of America are made on Form B; in periodicals, or in contributions thereto, manufactured outside the United States of America, except those subject to the ad interim provision of the copyright law, on Form A–B Foreign; and in periodicals, or in contributions thereto, in the English language manufactured and first published outside of the United States of America, and subject to the ad interim provisions of the copyright law, on Form A–B Ad Interim. Applications for registration of claims to copyright in contributions to periodicals manufactured in the United States of America are made on Form BB. Applications for registration of claims to copyright in contributions to periodicals, which contributions are prints published in connection with the sale or advertisement of an article or articles of merchandise, are made on Form KK.

§ 202.6 LECTURES OR SIMILAR PRODUCTIONS PREPARED FOR ORAL DELIVERY (CLASS C).

This class includes the scripts of unpublished works prepared in the first instance for oral delivery, such as lectures, sermons, addresses, monologs, panel discussions, and variety programs prepared for radio or television. The script submitted for registration in Class C should consist of the actual text of the works to be presented orally. Formats, outlines, brochures, synopses, or general descriptions of radio and television programs are not registrable in unpublished form. When published with notice as prescribed by law, such works may be considered for registration as "books" in Class A.

§ 202.7 DRAMATIC AND DRAMATICO-MUSICAL COMPOSITIONS (CLASS D).

This class includes published or unpublished works dramatic in character such as the acting version of plays for the stage, motion pictures, radio, television and the like, operas, operettas, musical comedies and similar productions, and pantomimes. Choreographic works of a dramatic character, whether the story or theme be expressed by music and action combined or by actions alone, are subject to registration in Class D. However, descriptions of dance steps and other physical gestures, including ballroom and social dances or choreographic works which do not tell a story, develop a character or emotion, or otherwise convey a dramatic concept or idea, are not subject to registration in Class D.

§ 202.8 MUSICAL COMPOSITIONS (CLASS E).

(a) This class includes published or unpublished musical compositions in the form of visible notation (other than dramatico-musical compositions), with or without words, as well as new versions of musical compositions, such as adaptations or arrangements, and editing when such editing is the writing of an author. The words of a song, when unaccompanied by music, are not registrable in Class E.

(b) A phonograph record or other sound recording is not considered a "copy" of the compositions recorded on it, and is not acceptable for copyright registration. Likewise, the Copyright Office does not register claims to exclusive rights in mechanical recordings themselves, or in the performances they reproduce.

§ 202.9 MAPS (CLASS F).

This class includes all published cartographic representations of area, such as terrestrial maps and atlases, marine charts, celestial maps and such three-dimensional works as globes and relief models.

§ 202.10 WORKS OF ART (CLASS G).

(a) *General.* This class includes published or unpublished works of artistic craftsmanship, insofar as their form but not their mechanical or utilitarian aspects are concerned, such as artistic jewelry, enamels, glassware, and tapestries, as well as works belonging to the fine arts, such as paintings, drawings and sculpture.

(b) In order to be acceptable as a work of art, the work must embody some creative authorship in its delineation or form. The registrability of a work of art is not affected by the intention of the author as to the use of the work, the number of copies reproduced, or the fact that it appears on a textile material or textile product. The potential availability of protection under the design patent law will not affect the registrability of a work of art, but a copyright claim in a patented design or in the drawings or photographs in a patent application will not be registered after the patent has been issued.

(c) If the sole intrinsic function of an article is its utility, the fact that the article is unique and attractively shaped will not qualify it as a work of art. However, if the shape of a utilitarian article incorporates features, such as artistic sculpture, carving, or pictorial representation, which can be identified separately and are capable of existing independently as a work of art, such features will be eligible for registration.

§ 202.11 REPRODUCTIONS OF WORKS OF ART (CLASS H).

This class includes published reproductions of existing works of art in the same or a different medium, such as a lithograph, photoengraving, etching, or drawing of a painting, sculpture or other work of art.

§ 202.12 DRAWINGS OR PLASTIC WORKS OF A SCIENTIFIC OR TECHNICAL CHARACTER (CLASS I).

(a) This class includes published or unpublished two-dimensional drawings and three-dimensional plastic works which have been designed for a scientific or technical use and which contain copyrightable graphic, pictorial, or sculptured material. Works registrable in Class I include diagrams or models illustrating scientific or technical works or formulating scientific or technical information in linear or plastic form, such as, for example: a mechanical drawing, an astronomical chart, an architect's blueprint, an anatomical model, or an engineering diagram.

(b) A work is not eligible for registration as a "plastic" work in Class I merely because it is formed from one of the commonly known synthetic chemical derivatives such as styrenes, vinyl compounds, or acrylic resins. The term "plastic work" as used in this context refers to a three-dimensional work giving the effect of that which is molded or sculptured. Examples of such works include statues of animals or plants used for scientific or educational purposes, and engineers' scale models.

(c) A claim to copyright in a scientific or technical drawing, otherwise registrable in Class I, will not be refused registration solely by reason of the fact that it is known to form a part of a pending patent application. Where the patent has been issued, however, the claim to copyright in the drawing will be denied copyright registration.

§ 202.13 PHOTOGRAPHS (CLASS J).

This class includes published or unpublished photographic prints and filmstrips, slide films and individual slides. Photoengravings and other photomechanical reproductions of photographs are registered in Class K on Form K.

§ 202.14 PRINTS, PICTORIAL ILLUSTRATIONS AND COMMERCIAL PRINTS OR LABELS (CLASS K).

(a) This class includes prints or pictorial illustrations, greeting cards, picture postcards and similar prints, produced by means of lithography, photoengraving or other methods of reproduction. These works when published are registered on Form K.

(b) A print or label, not a trademark, containing copyrightable pictorial matter, text, or both, published in connection with the sale or advertisement of an article or articles of merchandise is also registered in this class on Form KK. In the case of a print which is published in a periodical, use Form KK if the print is used in connection with the sale or advertisement of an article of merchandise, Form BB if it is not. Multipage works are more appropriately classified in Class A than in Class K.

(c) A claim to copyright cannot be registered in a print or label consisting solely of trademark subject matter and lacking copyrightable matter. While the Copyright Office will not investigate whether the matter has been or can be registered at the Patent Office, it will register a properly filed copyright claim in a print or label that contains the requisite qualifications for copyright even though there is a trademark on it. However, registration of a claim to copyright does not give the claimant rights available by trademark registrations at the Patent Office.

§ 202.15 MOTION PICTURES (CLASSES L–M).

A single application Form L–M is available for registration of works in Classes L (Motion-picture photoplays) and M (Motion pictures other than photoplays).

(a) *Photoplays (Class L)*. This class includes published or unpublished motion pictures that are dramatic in character and tell a connected story, such as feature films, filmed television plays, short subjects and animated cartoons having a plot.

(b) *Other than photoplays (Class M)*. This class includes published or unpublished nondramatic films such as newsreels, travelogs, training or promotional films, nature studies, and filmed television programs having no plot.

§202.16 DEPOSIT OF PHOTOGRAPHS OR OTHER IDENTIFYING REPRODUCTIONS IN LIEU OF COPIES.

(a) *Availability of option*. In the case of a published work which is reproduced in copies for sale, classified in Classes (g), (h), (i), and (k) of section 5, title 17, U.S. Code, copies of which are considered by the Register of Copyrights to be impracticable of deposit because of their size, weight, fragility, or monetary value, photographs or other identifying reproductions may be deposited in lieu of copies as provided by section 13, title 17, U.S. Code. The deposit of such photographs or reproductions shall be made in accordance with the following criteria:

(1) The number of sets of photographs or of reproductions to be submitted shall be the same as the number of copies provided by said section 13; duplicate sets shall be deposited unless the work is by a foreign author and has been published in a foreign country. Each set shall consist of as many photographs or reproductions in black and white, or in color, as are necessary to identify the work.

(2) All photographs or reproductions shall be of equal size, not less than 5 x 7 inches, and not exceeding 9 x 12 inches, but preferably 8 x 10 inches. The image of the work shown in all photographs or reproductions shall either be lifesize or larger, or if less than lifesize shall be at least 4 inches in its greatest dimension. The exact measurement of at least one dimension of the

work shall be indicated on at least one corresponding photograph or reproduction in each set.

(3) The copyright notice and its position on the work must be clearly shown on at least one corresponding photograph or reproduction in each set. If, because of the size or location of the copyright notice, a photographic reproduction cannot be prepared, a drawing may be included in each set, of the same size as the photographs or reproductions, showing the exact appearance of the notice, its dimensions, and its specific position on the work.

(4) The title of the work shall appear on the front or back of each photograph or reproduction.

(5) A copy shall be considered to be impracticable of deposit if, because of its size, weight, fragility or monetary value, it is unsuited to the filing procedures of the Copyright Office.

(b) *Exceptions.* The provisions of this section, permitting the deposit of photographs in lieu of copies in certain cases, shall not apply to fine prints and two-dimensional art reproductions. The Register of Copyrights reserves the right in any other particular case to require as a condition precedent to registration, the deposit of copies of the work as published.

§202.17 RENEWALS.

(a) Claims to renewal copyright must be registered within the last (28th) year of the original copyright term. The original term for a published work is computed from the date of first publication; the term for a work originally registered in unpublished form is computed from the date of registration in the Copyright Office. Unless the required application and fee are received in the Copyright Office during the prescribed period before the first term of copyright expires, copyright protection is lost permanently and the work enters the public domain. The Copyright Office has no discretion to extend the renewal time limits.

(b) Renewal claims may be registered only in the names of persons falling within one of the classes of renewal claimants specified in the copyright law. If the work was a new version of a previous work, renewal may be claimed only in the new matter.

§ 202.18 NOTICES OF USE.

Notices of use of copyrighted musical compositions on mechanical instruments, required by section 1(e) of title 17, U.S. Code, will be recorded upon receipt of a properly executed Form U and upon payment of the prescribed fees. Notices of intention to use will be received pursuant to section 101(e) of title 17, U.S. Code; no special form is provided therefor.

INDEX

A

I

J

L

T

Technical drawings or plastic works. *See* Drawings and plastic works of a scientific or technical character.

Terms of copyright (secs. 22–24), pp. 12, 13.

Time for taking action:

Ad interim copyright (secs. 22, 23), pp. 12, 13; (sec. 216), p. 26.

Assignments, recordation (sec. 30), p. 14; (sec. 216), p. 26.

Renewal copyright (secs. 24, 25), p. 13; (sec. 216), p. 26.

Transcriptions. *See* Records and transcriptions.

Transfer of copyright. *See* Assignment of copyright.

Translations (sec. 1b), p. 2; (sec. 7), p. 5.

Treasury, Department of. *See* Secretary of the Treasury.

Typesetting. *See* Manufacturing requirements.

U

United States Code:

Title 17, pp. 1–26.

Pertinent sections of Title 28, pp. 33–35.

Universal Copyright Convention:

Statement concerning, p. 42.

Text of, pp. 43–55.

U.S. law (sec. 9c), p. 7.

Unpublished works:

Common-law right (sec. 2), p. 4.

Deposit of copies (sec. 12), p. 8.

Destruction of (sec. 214), p. 25.

V

Virgin Islands, applicability of U.S. copyright laws in, p. 40.

W

Widow or widower of author may secure renewal copyright (sec. 24), p. 13.

Works of art. *See* Art, works of.

Writings of an author, subject-matter of copyright (sec. 4), p. 4.

Appendix 2

Change in Copyright Office Regulations

COPYRIGHT OFFICE
WASHINGTON, D.C. 20540

CHANGE IN COPYRIGHT OFFICE REGULATIONS

Section 202.17 of the Regulations of the Copyright Office (Chapter II of Title 37 of the *Code of Federal Regulations*), which relates to renewal applications, has been amended by the following provision which appeared in the April 1, 1970, issue of the *FEDERAL REGISTER*, Vol. 35, No. 63, at page 5402.

Title 37—PATENTS, TRADE-MARKS, AND COPYRIGHTS

Chapter II—Copyright Office, Library of Congress

PART 202—REGISTRATION OF CLAIMS TO COPYRIGHT

Renewal Applications

In confirmation of a procedure heretofore authorized and given effect by the Register of Copyrights in a number of cases, § 202.17 of Chapter II of Title 37 of the Code of Federal Regulations is amended by adding a new paragraph (c) reading as follows:

§ 202.17 Renewals.

* * * * *

(c) Whenever a renewal applicant has cause to believe that a formal application for renewal (form R), if sent to the Copyright Office by mail, might not be received in the Copyright Office before the expiration of the time limits provided by 17 U.S.C. section 24, he may apply for renewal registration by means of a telephone call, telegram, or other method of telecommunication. An application made by this method will be accepted if: (1) The message is received in the Copyright Office within the specified time limits; (2) the applicant adequately identifies the work involved, the date of first publication or original registration, the name and address of the renewal claimant, and the statutory basis of the renewal claim; and (3) the fee for renewal registration, if not already on deposit, is received in the Copyright Office before the time for renewal registration has expired.

(Sec. 207, 61 Stat. 666; 17 U.S.C. 207)

Dated: March 27, 1970.

ABRAHAM L. KAMINSTEIN
Register of Copyrights

Approved:

L. QUINCY MUMFORD
Librarian of Congress

[F.R. Doc. 70-3927; Filed, Mar. 31, 1970; 8:47 a.m.]

Appendix 3

Public Law 91-555—Joint Resolution

Public Law 91-555
91st Congress, S. J. Res. 230
December 17, 1970

Joint Resolution

84 STAT. 1441

Extending the duration of copyright protection in certain cases.

Resolved by the Senate and House of Representatives of the United States of America in Congress assembled, That in any case in which the renewal term of copyright subsisting in any work on the date of approval of this resolution, or the term thereof as extended by Public Law 87–668, by Public Law 89–442, by Public Law 90–141, by Public Law 90–416, or by Public Law 91–147 (or by all or certain of said laws), would expire prior to December 31, 1971, such term is hereby continued until December 31, 1971.

Approved December 17, 1970.

Copyright term, extension.

83 Stat. 360.
17 USC 24 notes.

LEGISLATIVE HISTORY:

HOUSE REPORT No. 91-1621 (Comm. on the Judiciary).
CONGRESSIONAL RECORD Vol. 116 (1970):
    Aug. 17, considered and passed Senate.
    Dec. 7, considered and passed House.

Appendix 4

"Patents, Trademarks, and Copyrights"—Report of the
Senate Subcommittee on Patents, Trademarks and Copyrights,
Ninety-First Congress, 1969–1970, with Extensive Reference
to S.543, the So-Called "Copyright Revision Bill"

91ST CONGRESS
2d Session

SENATE

{ REPORT
No. 91–1219

PATENTS, TRADEMARKS, AND COPYRIGHTS

R E P O R T

OF THE

COMMITTEE ON THE JUDICIARY
UNITED STATES SENATE

MADE BY ITS

SUBCOMMITTEE ON
PATENTS, TRADEMARKS, AND COPYRIGHTS

PURSUANT TO

S. Res. 49, Ninety-First Congress
First Session

SEPTEMBER 22, 1970.—Ordered to be printed

U.S. GOVERNMENT PRINTING OFFICE
48–008   WASHINGTON : 1970

COMMITTEE ON THE JUDICIARY

JAMES O. EASTLAND, Mississippi, *Chairman*

JOHN L. McCLELLAN, Arkansas
SAM J. ERVIN, JR., North Carolina
THOMAS J. DODD, Connecticut
PHILIP A. HART, Michigan
EDWARD M. KENNEDY, Massachusetts
BIRCH BAYH, Indiana
QUENTIN N. BURDICK, North Dakota
JOSEPH D. TYDINGS, Maryland
ROBERT C. BYRD, West Virginia

EVERETT McKINLEY DIRKSEN, Illinois [1]
ROMAN L. HRUSKA, Nebraska
HIRAM L. FONG, Hawaii
HUGH SCOTT, Pennsylvania
STROM THURMOND, South Carolina
MARLOW W. COOK, Kentucky
CHARLES McC. MATHIAS, JR., Maryland
ROBERT P. GRIFFIN, Michigan [2]

SUBCOMMITTEE ON PATENTS, TRADEMARKS, AND COPYRIGHTS

JOHN L. McCLELLAN, Arkansas, *Chairman*

PHILIP A. HART, Michigan
QUENTIN N. BURDICK, North Dakota

HUGH SCOTT, Pennsylvania
HIRAM L. FONG, Hawaii

THOMAS C. BRENNAN, *Chief Counsel*
EDD N. WILLIAMS, Jr., *Assistant Counsel*

[1] Senator Dirksen died Sept. 7, 1969.

[2] On Sept. 17, 1969, by resolution of the Senate (S. Res. 256), Hon. Robert P. Griffin was assigned to serve on this committee.

(II)

PATENTS, TRADEMARKS AND COPYRIGHTS

September 22, 1970.—Ordered to be printed

Mr. McClellan, from the Committee on the Judiciary,
submitted the following

REPORT

[Pursuant to S. Res. 49, 91st Cong., first sess., as extended]

Introduction

During the first session of the 91st Congress, pursuant to Senate Resolution 49, which was approved on February 7, 1969, the Standing Subcommittee on Patents, Trademarks and Copyrights was authorized to "conduct a full and complete examination and review of the administration of the Patent Office and a complete examination and review of the statutes relating to patents, trademarks, and copyrights." To enable the subcommittee to carry out its duties under the resolution, the Senate authorized expenditures of $105,000 for the period between February 1, 1969 and January 31, 1970. By a careful handling of the monies appropriated, the subcommittee was not required to seek additional funds from the Senate last year to cover the increased salaries authorized by the July pay bill and was able to return approximately $1,000 to the contingent fund of the Senate at the expiration of the resolution.

The Judiciary Committee in 1969 referred to the subcommittee twenty-three bills in which the subject matter thereof pertained to patents, trademarks or copyrights. The activities of the subcommittee last year included the study of and evaluation of these measures. Among the legislation referred to the subcommittee were bills to provide for the general revision of both the copyright law and patent law, private relief measures in the field of patent law, bills to amend the trademark statutes to provide for a Federal law of unfair competition and legislation to extend the duration of copyright protection in certain cases. Several of these measures were acted upon by the subcommittee during the first session of this Congress. The activities of the subcommittee also included the providing of assistance by the staff to Members of the Senate on matters relating to patents, trademarks and copyrights.

LEGISLATION

1. Legislation reported during the first session by the subcommittee, approved by the Committee on the Judiciary, passed by the Senate and the House of Representatives, and approved by the President.

Public Law 91–147 (S.J. Res. 143, McClellan), to extend the duration of copyright protection in certain cases.

The purpose of this legislation was to continue until December 31, 1970, the renewal term of any copyright subsisting on the date of approval of this resolution or the term as extended by Public Laws 87–688, 89–142, 90–141, or 90–416 (or by all or any of said laws) where such term would otherwise expire prior to December 31, 1970. The purpose of the extension was to continue the renewal term of copyrights pending the enactment by the Congress of a general revision of the copyright laws, including a proposed increase in the length of the copyright term.

Senate Joint Resolution 143 (Public Law 91–147) was the fifth resolution passed by the Congress providing for the interim extension of copyright. The fourth extension (Public Law 90–416) expired December 31, 1969. This legislation merely provides for the prolongation of the renewal term of the copyright and does not involve creation of a new term of copyright.

This legislation was passed by the Senate on October 6, 1969, and by the House of Representatives on December 1, 1969. It was approved by the President on December 16, 1969. This legislation is discussed in greater detail in Senate Report No. 91–447 of the first session of the 91st Congress.

2. Legislation reported by the subcommittee, approved by the Committee on the Judiciary and passed by the Senate, but not approved by the House of Representatives.

S. 497 (Cotton), for the relief of Capt. John N. Laycock, U.S. Navy (retired).

The purpose of this legislation was to pay to the estate of Capt. John N. Laycock, U.S. Navy (retired), formerly of Derry, N. H., the sum of $170,000, which sum shall be considered a payment in consideration of a transfer by the estate of Capt. John N. Laycock, U.S. Navy (retired), of property consisting of all substantial rights to a patent within the meaning of section 1235 of the Internal Revenue Code of 1954, in full settlement for the usage by the United States during and subsequent to World War II of certain pontoon equipment patented by him (U.S. No. 2,480,144), and for losses incurred by the said Capt. John N. Laycock as a result of the United States having made such pontoon equipment, and the patent thereto, available to other nations contrary to the license agreement entered into between the United States and the said Capt. Laycock. The bill provided for a limitation of 10 percent on attorneys' fees.

The committee reported S. 497 on November 18, 1969. It was passed by the Senate on November 26, 1969.

A more complete statement of the committee's views is contained in Senate Report No. 532 of the first session of the 91st Congress.

3. Legislation reported by the subcommittee, but no action taken by the Committee or the Judiciary.

S. 543 (McClellan), to provide for the general revision of the copyright law, title 17 of the United States Code, and for other purposes.

This legislation is discussed in greater detail elsewhere in the report.

S. 1774 (Hart), to encourage the creation of original ornamental designs of useful articles by protecting the authors of such designs for a limited time against unauthorized copying.

This legislation is discussed in greater detail elsewhere in the report.

4. Legislation pending in the Subcommittee at the adjournment of the first session of the 91st Congress.

S. 766 (McClellan, for himself and Mr. Scott), to amend the Trademark Act to provide for the registration and protection of trademarks used in commerce, to carry out the provisions of certain international conventions, and for other purposes. This bill is known as the Unfair Competition Act of 1969.

S. 877 (Tydings), for the relief of John S. Attinello.

S. 879 (Tydings), for the relief of the estate of Albert W. Small.

S. 1008 (Hart), for the relief of Robert J. Ebbert and Design Products Corporation, Troy, Michigan.

S. 1064 (Bayh), to provide for the extension of the term of certain patents of persons who served in the military forces of the United States.

S. 1237 (Pell), for the relief of Ralph R. Turner.

S. 1238 (Pell), for the relief of Oresto A. Minardi and Dickran Manoogian.

S. 1246 (McClellan), for the general revision of the Patent Laws, title 35 of the United States Code, and for other purposes.

S. 1249 (Fannin), for the relief of Bert N. Adams and Emma Adams.

S. 1568 (Dirksen), to amend the Act entitled "An Act to provide for the registration and protection of trademarks used in commerce, to carry out the provisions of international conventions, and for other purposes," approved July 5, 1946, as amended.

S. 1569 (Dirksen), for the promotion of the progress of the useful arts by the general revision of the Patent Laws, title 35 of the United states Code, and for other purposes.

S. 1983 (Tydings), for the relief of Commander Frederick J. Lewis, Junior, United states Navy (retired).

S. 2756 (McClellan), for the general revision of the Patent Laws, title 35 of the United states Code, and for other purposes.

S. 2845 (Baker), for the relief of George W. Hardin.

S. 3051 (Fannin, for himself and Mr. Hart), to extend Letters Patent Numbered 2,322,210, and for other purposes.

S. 3109 (McClellan, by request), to amend section 6 of title 35, United states Code, "Patents," to authorize domestic and international studies and programs relating to patents and trademarks.

S. 2110 (McClellan, by request), to amend the Act entitled "An Act to provide for the registration and protection of trademarks used in commerce, to carry out the provisions of international conventions, and for other purposes", approved July 5, 1946, as amended.

S. 3168 (Brooke), for the relief of Daniel H. Robbins.

H.R. 7567 (Udall), for the relief of Bert N. Adams and Emma Adams.

4

CopyRIGHT LAW REVISION

The most significant development in 1969 in the field of copyright law revision was the approval of legislation by the subcommittee to provide for the first general revision of the copyright laws and procedures since 1909. As the subcommittee had concluded its extensive hearings on this subject in the 90th Congress, it was able last year to complete action on S. 543, the current copyright revision legislation. The subcommittee reported S. 543 with amendments to the full Judiciary Committee on December 10th with a recommendation that it be approved. It is anticipated that the Judiciary Committee will consider the bill in early 1970.

Senator John L. McClellan, Chairman of the Subcommittee, introduced S. 543 on January 22, 1969. Other than for necessary technical amendments, relating principally to the effective dates of certain provisions, this bill is identical to S. 597 which Senator McClellan introduced in the 90th Congress at the request of the Librarian of Congress. The bill, as introduced, contained two titles. Title I provides for the general revision of the copyright statutes and procedures and contains the vast majority of the bill's many complicated and controversial provisions. Title II provides for the establishment in the Library of Congress of a National Commission on New Technological Uses of Copyrighted Works. During consideration of the bill, the subcommittee amended it to provide for title III. Title III provides for the Protection of Ornamental Designs of Useful Articles. A brief summary of the major provisions contained in each of the bill's three titles is included in this report.

TITLE I

REVISION OF COPYRIGHT STATUTES AND PROCEDURES

1. Subject matter of copyright

Under the bill, the subject matter of copyright is original works of authorship fixed in any tangible medium of expression, now known or later developed, from which they can be preceived, reproduced, or otherwise communicated, either directly or with the aid of a machine or device. The measure retains the present categories of copyrightable works and includes protection for the first time to sound recordings. S. 543 also specifies that the United States Government is prohibited from securing a copyright in any of its publications.

2. Single system of copyright protection

The bill abolishes the present dual system of common law protection for unpublished works and the Federal law protection for published works. The measure establishes a single system of Federal statutory protection for all works covered by the bill regardless of whether they are published or unpublished. S. 543 does not, however, abolish or limit any rights or remedies under the common law or statutes of any State with respect to unpublished works not protected by the bill, or any cause of action arising from undertakings commenced before January 1, 1971, or any activities violating rights that are not equivalent to any of the exclusive rights within the general scope of copyright as specified by the legislation.

3. Duration of copyright

Under the current law, the term of copyright is twenty-eight years from first publication or registration plus another twenty-eight years if the copyright is renewed. The bill changes this term of protection and provides in general that works created after the effective date of this legislation shall endure for a term consisting of the life of the author and fifty years after his death. With respect to joint works, the fifty years is computed from the death of the last surviving author. In the case of anonymous works, pseudonymous works, or works made for hire, the measure specifies that the term shall consist of seventy-five years from the year of its first publication, or a term of one hundred years from the year of its creation, whichever expires first. Regarding works now protected, the legislation provides that copyrights subsisting in their first term shall endure for twenty-eight years from the date it was originally secured with renewal rights for a further term of forty-seven years. For copyrights in their renewal term, the bill extends the duration of protection to seventy-five years from the date the copyright was originally secured.

4. Exclusive rights in copyrighted works

The bill provides the owner of a copyrighted work five exclusive rights. Under the measure, a copyright owner is given the exclusive right to, (1) reproduce the work in copies or phonorecords, (2) prepare derivative works based upon the work, (3) distribute copies or phonorecords of the work, (4) perform the work publicly, and (5) display the work publicly. The bill specifies, however, that certain limitations shall apply to these rights.

5. Fair use

The doctrine of fair use is one of the most important limitations on the copyright owners' exclusive rights. The fair-use limitation, which is a judicially developed doctrine, permits a limited amount of copying without it being an infringement of copyright. The bill provides for the first statutory recognition of the doctrine and specifies that the fair use of a copyrighted work, including the reproduction of copies for purposes of teaching or research is not a copyright infringement. In determining whether the doctrine applies to a particular case, the bill specifies that four factors are to be considered. These factors are the purpose and character of the use, the nature of the work, the amount of the work used and the effect of the use upon the potential market or value of the copyrighted work.

6. Reproduction by libraries and archives

Another of the limitations on a copyright owners' exclusive rights is the reproduction of copyrighted works by libraries and archives. The bill provides that under certain conditions it is not an infringement of copyright for a library or archives to reproduce or distribute no more than one copy or phonorecord of a work. The reproduction or distribution must not be for any commercial advantage and the collections of the library or archives must be available to the public or to other persons doing research in a specialized field. The measure also specifies that the reproduction or distribution of an unpublished work must be for the purpose of preservation and security, or for deposit for research use in another library or archives. The bill further provides that the reproduction of a published work must be for the purposes of replacement of a copy that is damaged, deteriorating, lost, or stolen, and that the library or archives has determined that an unused replacement cannot be obtained at a normal price from commonly-known trade sources in the United States. The rights given to the libraries and archives by this provision of the bill are in addition to those granted under the fair-use doctrine.

7. *Jukebox exemption*

The bill repeals the present exemption of jukebox operators from payment of performance royalties for use of copyrighted musical compositions or coin-operated phonorecord players. When Congress enacted the 1909 copyright law, it specifically exempted jukebox operators from the payment of such fees. During the sixty-one years the exemption has been in effect, the jukebox operators have been the only commercial users of copyrighted music not required to pay performance royalties.

Although the measure repeals the jukebox exemption, it does provide for a system of compulsory licensing. Under the bill, if a jukebox operator does not desire a negotiated license, he may obtain a compulsory license by complying with certain reporting requirements and paying a statutory royalty fee of $9 per year per phonorecord. The bill specifies that the fees shall be paid to the Register of Copyrights who shall distribute one-ninth of the royalties to the copyright owners and performers of sound recordings, and the remainder to owners of copyright in nondramatic musical works. The measure further provides that failure to comply with the terms of the compulsory license shall render the jukebox operator fully liable as an infringer.

8. *Manufacturing clause*

The bill retains the essential features of manufacturing clause of the current law which requires, with certain exceptions, that an English language book or periodical must be manufactured in the United States in order to be fully protected under the copyright law. This provision of the law is commonly known as the manufacturing requirement and was enacted by Congress in 1891 to protect the printing industry of this country from foreign competition, which was based on substantially lower wage rates.

Although the measure provides for a manufacturing requirement, it does make substantial changes designed to narrow the scope of the requirement and to prevent it from causing technical forfeitures. Instead of the complete loss of protection that can result from violation of the present law, the bill provides for the possible loss of certain rights against infringers. The measure also increases the number of copies of a foreign edition that could be imported without violation of the requirement from 1,500 to 2,000. The bill further specified that Canada is exempted from the provisions of the manufacturing clause.

9. *Mechanical Royalty Rate*

The existing law provides that once the copyright owner of a musical work has permitted its use on a phonorecord, anyone else may also record the work upon notifying the copyright owner and paying a royalty of two cents for each composition recorded. S. 543 retains the compulsory licensing feature of the current law, but increases the royalty rate to two and a half cents or one-half cent per minute of playing time on each phonorecord, whichever is larger. The bill also specified that failure to obtain either a negotiated or compulsory license, or a default in payment under a compulsory license, renders the user fully liable as an infringer.

During consideration of the measure, the subcommittee amended it to provide that royalties be paid only on records made and distributed. The subcommittee also rejected an amendment offered by Senator Philip A. Hart to provide that the royalty rate be eight percent of the manufacturer's suggested retail price of the record. The majority felt that eight percent was too high and that the merchandising practices of the record industry would make it difficult to relate the royalty to a suggested retail price.

10. Performance rights in sound recordings

S. 543, as introduced, specifically denied to the copyright owner the exclusive right of public performance in sound recordings, even though sound recordings were afforded protection for the first time under the copyright laws. This protection, however, was limited to the unauthorized duplication and the distribution of sound recordings without the authority of the copyright owner. Without the exclusive right of public performance in sound recordings, the copyright owner is unable to receive royalties for the public performance of his recorded work by anyone else.

During consideration of the legislation, the subcommittee approved a modified version of an amendment submitted by Senator Harrison A. Williams, of New Jersey, to provide for the establishment of performance rights in sound recordings. The amendment adopted divides the ownership of performance rights between the record producers and the performers, and also subjects such rights to a system of compulsory licensing. Under the measure, the fees would be paid to the Copyright Office which would issue regulations for their distribution among the claimants.

The legislation provides that the royalties may, at the user's option, be computed on either a blanket or a prorated basis. For a radio or television station, the blanket rate is two percent of the net receipts received from advertising sponsors. The prorated rate is a fraction of two percent of such net receipts, based on a calculation made in accordance with a standard formula that the Register of Copyrights shall prescribe by regulation, taking into account the amount of the station's commercial time devoted to playing copyrighted sound recordings and whether the station is a radio or television broadcaster. For companies that supply background music and other transmitters of performances of sound recordings, the blanket rate is two percent of the gross receipts received from subscribers or others who pay to receive the transmissions. The prorated rate for background music companies is computed by the Register of Copyrights under a formula similar to that used in calculating the prorated rate for radio and television stations. The measure also exempts broadcast stations and background music companies whose gross annual receipts are less than $25,000 and $10,000 respectively from the payment of royalties for the use of sound recordings. The bill further specifies that cable systems and jukebox operators shall also pay performance royalties for the use of phonorecords. The bill further provides that performers on phonorecords include musicians, singers, conductors, actors, narrators, and others whose performance of a literary, musical, or dramatic work is embodied in sound recording.

11. *Educational broadcasting*

Under the current law, the broadcasting of a copyrighted non-dramatic literary or musical work is not an infringement of copyright unless it is for profit. The bill removes this blanket exemption and provides for full liability for all transmissions of copyrighted material except those of governmental bodies or nonprofit educational institutions made primarily for reception in classrooms.

The measure specifies that the exemption applies only to the performance of a nondramatic literary or musical work, or of a sound recording, or display of a work. The legislation further requires that three conditions be met before the transmission of such works is exempted from copyright liability. These conditions are that the performance of display is (1) a regular part of the systematic instructional activities of a governmental body or a nonprofit educational institution, (2) directly related and of material assistance to the teaching content of the transmission, and (3) the transmission is made primarily for reception, (A) in classrooms or similar places normally devoted to instruction or (B) by persons to whom the transmission is directed because their disabilities or other special circumstances prevent their attendance in classrooms or similar places normally devoted to instruction, or (C) by officers or employees of governmental bodies as a part of their official duties or employment.

12. *Cable systems*

During its study of this legislation, the subcommittee considered many important and controversial issues. None was more complicated, however, than the issue pertaining to the retransmission of primary broadcast signals by cable systems. The CATV issue was even more difficult to resolve because certain aspects of it were regulatory in nature and therefore outside the jurisdiction of the subcommittee. Consequently, the bill does not contain provisions relating to such subjects as program origination by cable systems, advertising or the application to cable systems of Federal Communications Commission requirements in the area of technical standards. However, the measure does include provisions pertaining to other phases of the issue, such as the payment and distribution of copyright fees by cable systems and the importation of distant television signals transmitting copyright programs.

The bill provides that nothing in this legislation shall deny the public the opportunity to receive those signals and programs being received prior to January 1, 1971, in accordance with the regulations of the Federal Communications Commission or any other governmental agency shall not issue or enforce any regulation requiring a cable system to obtain authority of the copyright owner as a condition for making any secondary transmission, or prohibiting a cable system from making secondary transmissions within an area where such transmissions are permissible under this legislation.

In developing the CATV provision of the bill, the subcommittee felt that each community in the United States is entitled to adequate television service. In the top 50 broadcasting markets, the bill provides that adequate television service shall consist of the reception of the three major national networks, three independent commercial stations and one noncommercial educational station. In markets below the top 50, the measure provides that adequate television service shall consist of the reception of the three major national networks, two independent commercial stations and one noncommercial educational station. The legislation also specifies that a cable system may import such distant signals under a compulsory license as are necessary to provide adequate television service. In order to receive the compulsory license, however, the cable system must carry the closest signal of any other station of the same type whose lack deprives that market of adequate television service.

The legislation establishes a system of compulsory licensing for cable systems. The measure provides that the secondary transmission by a cable system of a primary transmission embodying a copyrighted work is subject to compulsory licensing if (1) the signals comprising the primary transmissions are exclusively aural, or (2) the reference point of a cable system is within the local service area of the primary transmitter, or (3) the reference point of a cable system is outside any U.S. television market, as defined by the bill. If one of these conditions exist, the bill provides that a cable system may secure a compulsory license upon complying with certain reporting requirements and paying the necessary copyright fees.

The bill requires every cable system transmitting secondary signals under a compulsory license to pay copyright fees. The measure provides for a graduated fee schedule and specifies that a cable system shall pay copyright royalties of (1) one percent of any gross receipts up to $40,000; (2) two percent of any gross receipts totalling more than $40,000, but not more than $80,000; (3) three percent of any gross receipts totalling more than $80,000, but not more than $120,000; (4) four percent of any gross receipts totalling more than $120,000, but not more than $160,000; and (5) five percent of any gross receipts totalling more than $160,000. The legislation also requires a cable system to pay an additional royalty of one percent of its gross receipts for each signal transmitted above the number of signals necessary to constitute adequate service. The copyright fees are to be paid quarterly to the Register of Copyrights who in turn will distribute the funds to the copyright owners.

The legislation also subjects a cable system to full copyright liability for its secondary transmissions where a primary broadcaster has acquired the exclusive right to transmit any performance of a work, and (1) the reference point of a cable system falls within a radius of 35 air miles from the center of a United States television market; and (2) the primary transmission is made by a television station whose local service area is outside the market; and (3) the market is one of the first 50 of the United States television markets; and (4) the station having the exclusive right has given written notice of the right to the cable system within the time limits prescribed by the Register of Copyrights. The measure further provides that if all of the preceding conditions are present but the market in which the cable system is functioning is below the top 50 television markets, then the cable system is required to refrain from transmitting the work covered by the exclusive license of the local broadcaster only if such work has never been transmitted to the public in a syndicated showing in that market.

13. Copyright Royalty Tribunal

The bill establishes in the Library of Congress a Copyright Royalty Tribunal to adjust royalty rates paid to copyright owners by users of copyrighted works under the various systems of compulsory licensing created under the measure. The subcommittee felt that it would not be sound public policy to require that an Act of Congress be enacted every time an adjustment of one of these rates is desired.

The measure provides that any owner or user of a copyrighted work whose royalty rates are specified in the provisions relating to cable television and performance rights in sound recordings may file a petition with the Tribunal in 1974 and in each subsequent fifth year requesting that these rates be opened for review and possible adjustment. The bill also provides for the filing of a similar petition in 1976 and in each subsequent fifth year by any owner or user of a copyrighted work whose royalty rates are specified in the provisions relating to the making and distribution of phonorecords and the public performance of records on coin-operated phonorecord players. If it is determined that the petitioner has sufficient standing the Tribunal would conduct such studies and take such testimony as it deems necessary. The measure further provides that the Librarian of Congress, with the concurrence of the parties, shall select the members of the Tribunal from a panel nominated by the American Arbitration Association. If the Tribunal determines that an adjustment in any statutory rate is warranted the judgment shall not become effective for six months. If either House of Congress during that period passes a resolution disapproving the decision of the Tribunal, there would be no adjustment of the rate and the matter could not be further considered until five years later.

Title II

NATIONAL COMMISSION ESTABLISHED

The language in Title II, as introduced, is identical to that contained in S. 2216 approved by the Senate in the first session of the 90th Congress. The provisions of Title II establishes in the Library of Congress a National Commission on New Technological Uses of Copyrighted Works to study and compile data on the reproduction and use of copyrighted works of authorship (1) in automatic systems capable of storing, processing, retrieving, and transferring information, and (2) by various forms of machine reproduction. The measure further provides that the Commission shall make recommendations as to such changes in copyrighted law or procedures that may be necessary to assure for such purposes access to copyrighted works, and to provide recognition of the rights of the copyright owners.

Title II, as introduced, also specified that the Commission shall be composed of 23 members, consisting of a Chairman who shall be the Librarian of Congress, two Members of the Senate, two Members of the House of Representatives, seven members appointed by the President selected from authors and other copyright owners, seven members appointed by the President selected from users of copyrighted works, and four nongovernmental members appointed by the President selected from the public generally. It further required that the Senate must advise and consent to the nominations of the 18 members selected by the President. The measure also provided for the selection by the Commission of one of its members as Vice Chairman and specified that the Register of Copyrights shall serve as an ex officio member of the Commission.

During the subcommittee's consideration of Title II, concern was expressed over the scope of the Commission's study. In order to clarify the intent of the subcommittee, the measure was amended to provide that the study of the reproduction of copyrighted works by various forms of machine reproduction did not include reproduction by or at the request of instructors for use in face-to-face teaching activities. Title II was also amended to assure that the Commission's study was to include the creating of new works by the application or intervention of such automatic systems or machine reproduction.

The Subcommittee also amended Title II to provide that the Commission shall be composed of thirteen members consisting of the Librarian of Congress and twelve members appointed by the President without the advice and consent of the Senate. The twelve members appointed by the President shall consist of four selected from authors and other copyright owners, four selected from users of copyrighted works and four nongovernmental members selected from the public generally. The measure was further amended to provide that the President shall appoint the Chairman and Vice Chairman and that seven members of the Commission shall constitute a quorum. The remaining provisions of Title II are miscellaneous in nature and relate to such functions as the financing of the Commission, the filling of vacancies on the Commission, and its term which is 3 years from the effective date of the legislation.

TITLE III

PROTECTION OF ORNAMENTAL DESIGNS

During consideration of S. 543 by the Subcommittee, it was amended to provide for the protection of ornamental designs of useful articles. The language in Title III is identical to S. 1774, introduced by Senator Philip A. Hart on April 3, 1969, and to S. 1237 passed by the Senate during the second session of the 89th Congress. Title III is also substantially similar to S. 1884 approved by the Senate in the 87th Congress, and S. 775 passed by the Senate in the 88th Congress.

The purpose of the legislation contained in Title III is to encourage the creation of original ornamental designs of useful articles by protecting the authors of such designs for a limited time against unauthorized copying. The legislation is intended to offer the creators of ornamental designs of useful articles a new form of protection directed toward the special problems arising in the design field, and is intended to avoid the defects of the existing copy-right and design patent statutes by providing simple, easily secured, and effective design protection for the period of 5 years, or, if renewed, a period of 10 years, under appropriate safeguards and conditions.

Because of its favorable action on Title III, the subcommittee reported S. 1774 back to the Judiciary Committee with a recommendation for indefinite postponement.

PATENT LAW REVISION

During this session the Subcommittee also continued its consideration of several bills providing for a general revision of the patent laws and procedures. The Subcommittee completed hearings on this subject in the 90th Congress, but delayed reporting a bill at the request of the Patent Bar in order to permit additional time for study.

Senator John L. McClellan, introduced S. 1246 a bill to provide for a general revision of the patent system on February 28, 1969. The bill reflects a distillation of the various bills and proposals for patent law reform considered by the Subcommittee during the previous Congress. Most significant of the changes is the redrafting of Section 102(g) to eliminate the language requiring the applicant for a patent to exercise continuous reasonable diligence leading to the making of the invention available to the public, and the elimination of the two year limitation on the proof that may be introduced in a patent invalidity contest. The bill also provides authority for the Commissioner of Patents to exchange all publications of the Patent Office and to furnish publications to international organizations. In addition, the measure reduces the length of time in which an applicant has to pay the final issue fee from nine to six months. The bill further provides for the removal of the distinction between contributory and direct infringement.

On August 1, Senator McClellan again introduced legislation to provide for reform of the patent system. The measure, S. 2756, incorporates a number of proposals recommended by the new Commissioner of Patents and various patent bar associations. At the request of the administration, however, the Subcommittee delayed further action on the bill in order to allow the executive branch time to determine its position on certain aspects of the legislation.

The legislation provides for the clarification of certain language in section 103 of the present law, and includes several guidelines to assist the Patent Office and the courts in interpreting the required standard of patentability. In introducing S. 2756, Senator McClellan stated, "It is not the purpose of the revised section 103 to lower the conditions of patentability which have traditionally been required by statute in pursuance of the limited constitutional grant of power to the Congress. The revised 103 should contribute to a reduction in the divergencies and uncertainties which have arisen in the various circuits and promote the orderly development of a consistent standard of patentability. It is to be hoped that these changes will result also in fewer reversals of Federal district court decisions by courts of appeals, and the giving of greater weight to the findings of those courts which have had the opportunity to hear the testimony and observe the witnesses."

Under the current patent statute, an applicant is entitled to a patent upon compliance with certain conditions. However, the statute is silent as to whether the applicant or the Patent Office bears the burden of proof in satisfying these conditions. The bill amends the current statute to provide that the burden of proof shall rest on the applicant. The bill also provides the Commissioner of Patents with authority to issue regulations requiring the applicant to cite the prior art considered in the preparation of his application.

Section 104 of the present patent law prohibits a foreign patent applicant from relying on foreign inventive activities in establishing a date of invention. Since this section discriminates against such applicants, the President's Commission on the Patent System recommended its repeal and the proposal was included in earlier patent bills introduced by Senator McClellan. At the request of the present Commissioner of Patent, however, section 104 is retained in S. 2756.

Another recommendation made by the President's Commission was to include in patent reform legislation language clarifying the licensing of patent rights field-of-use restrictions and the doctrine of patent misuse. The Commission's recommendation was not included in the previous administration's patent revision bill. The Antitrust Division of the Department of Justice has consistently opposed the incorporation of this proposal in any patent legislation. The Justice Department takes the view that any necessary development or clarification of the law in this area could be obtained as part of its antitrust enforcement program. Consequently no provisions on this subject are included in the bill.

In 1965 Congress passed legislation revising the patent fee schedule. Based on the present fee schedule, the Patent Office is supposed to recover between 65% and 75% of its operating cost through patent fees. S. 2756 retains the present fee schedule and provides that the Patent Office shall normally recover 65% of its cost. It also directs the Commissioner of Patents to transmit his recommendations for adjustment of the fee schedule whenever the recovery rate consistently falls below 65%. The Department of Commerce in 1969 recommended that the adjustment of such fees be considered in separate legislation and indicated they would later transmit their recommendations to the Congress. It is anticipated that such recommendations will be submitted during the second session of the 91st Congress.

The measure also strengthens the presumption of patent validity by providing that a party challenging the validity of a patent under section 103 has the burden of establishing obviousness of the claimed invention by clear and convincing evidence. The measure further provides that the Federal patent statute does not preempt contractual or other rights or obligations not in the nature of patent rights imposed by State or Federal law on particular parties with regard to inventions or discoveries, whether or not subject to title 35.

The legislation does not provide for any major statutory changes in the current patent examination procedures. The Patent Office advised the Subcommittee that legislative changes in this area would not be necessary because the goal of a more rapid disposal of patent applications could be obtained by various administrative actions. The Patent Office indicated that by fiscal year 1972 the pendency period of patent applications would be reduced from the recent average of thirty months to eighteen months. The new Commissioner of Patents in testifying before the Senate Judiciary Committee on May 2, 1969, assured the committee that he would take appropriate measures to implement this program. On the basis of the assurances made by the Commissioner of Patents, Senator McClellan decided that the bill should not contain provisions providing for any major modifications of the present examination procedures.

The Subcommittee in 1969 also considered one other patent reform bill. On March 17, 1969, the late Senator Everett M. Dirksen introduced S. 1569 to provide for the promotion of the progress of the useful arts by the general revision of the patent laws, and for other purposes.

○

Appendix 5

Facsimile of Application for Registration of a Claim to
Copyright

Page 1

FORM A

𝕬pplication for 𝕽egistration of a 𝕮laim to 𝕮opyright
in a published book manufactured in the United States of America

CLASS	REGISTRATION NO.
A	DO NOT WRITE HERE

Instructions: Make sure that all applicable spaces have been completed before you submit the form. The application must be **SIGNED** at line 10 and the **AFFIDAVIT** (line 11) **must be COMPLETED AND NOTARIZED.** The application should not be submitted until after the date of publication given in line 4, and should state the facts which existed on that date. For further information, see page 4.

Pages 1 and 2 should be typewritten or printed with pen and ink. Pages 3 and 4 should contain exactly the same information as pages 1 and 2, but may be carbon copies. Mail all pages of the application to the Register of Copyrights, Library of Congress, Washington, D.C. 20540, together with 2 copies of the best edition of the work and the registration fee of $6. Make your remittance payable to the Register of Copyrights.

1. Copyright Claimant(s) and Address(es): Give the name(s) and address(es) of the copyright owner(s). Ordinarily the name(s) should be the same as in the notice of copyright on the copies deposited.

Name ....

Address ....

Name ....

Address ....

2. Title: ....
(Give the title of the book as it appears on the title page)

....

3. Authors: Citizenship and domicile information must be given. Where a work was made for hire, the employer is the author. The citizenship of organizations formed under U.S. Federal or State law should be stated as U.S.A. Authors may be editors, compilers, translators, illustrators, etc., as well as authors of original text. If the copyright claim is based on new matter (see line 5) give requested information about the author of the new matter.

Name .... Citizenship ....
(Give legal name followed by pseudonym if latter appears on the copies) (Name of country)

Domiciled in U.S.A. Yes .... No .... Address ....

Name .... Citizenship ....
(Give legal name followed by pseudonym if latter appears on the copies) (Name of country)

Domiciled in U.S.A. Yes .... No .... Address ....

Name .... Citizenship ....
(Give legal name followed by pseudonym if latter appears on the copies) (Name of country)

Domiciled in U.S.A. Yes .... No .... Address ....

4. Date of Publication of This Edition: Give the complete date when copies of this particular edition were first placed on sale, sold, or publicly distributed. The date when copies were made or printed should not be confused with the date of publication. **NOTE:** The full date (month, day, and year) must be given. For further information, see page 4.

....
(Month)   (Day)   (Year)

➤➤➤ **(NOTE: Leave line 5 blank unless the following instructions apply to this work.)** ◀◀◀

5. New Matter in This Version: If any substantial part of this work has been previously published anywhere, give a brief, general statement of the nature of the new matter published for the first time in this version. New matter may consist of compilation, translation, abridgment, editorial revision, and the like, as well as additional text or pictorial matter.

....

....

➤➤➤ **NOTE:** | Leave line 6 blank unless there has been a PREVIOUS FOREIGN EDITION in the English language. | ◀◀◀

6. Book in English Previously Manufactured and Published Abroad: If all or a substantial part of the text of this edition was previously manufactured and published abroad in the English language, complete the following spaces:

Date of first publication of foreign edition .... (Year)   Was registration for the foreign edition made in the U.S. Copyright Office? Yes .... No ....

If your answer is "Yes," give registration number ....

EXAMINER

Complete all applicable spaces on next page

7. If registration fee is to be charged to a deposit account established in the Copyright Office, give name of account:

....

8. Name and address of person or organization to whom correspondence or refund, if any, should be sent:

Name .... Address ....

9. Send certificate to:

(Type or print name and address)

Name ....

Address ....
(Number and street)

....
(City) (State) (ZIP code)

10. Certification: (NOTE: Application not acceptable unless signed)
I CERTIFY that the statements made by me in this application are correct to the best of my knowledge.

....
(Signature of copyright claimant or duly authorized agent)

11. Affidavit (required by law.) Instructions: (1) Fill in the blank spaces with special attention to those marked **"(X)."** (2) Sign the affidavit before an officer authorized to administer oaths within the United States, such as a notary public. (3) Have the officer sign and seal the affidavit and fill in the date of execution.
NOTE: The affidavit must be signed and notarized only *on or after* the date of publication or completion of printing which it states. The affidavit *must* be signed by an individual.

STATE OF ....

COUNTY OF ....

ss:

I, the undersigned, depose and say that I am the
☐ Person claiming copyright in the book described in this application;
☐ Duly authorized agent of the person or organization claiming copyright in the book described in this application;
☐ Printer of the book described in this application.

That the book was published or the printing was completed on: **(X)** ....
(Give month, day, and year)

That, of the various processes employed in the production of the copies deposited, the setting of the type was performed within the limits of the United States or the making of the plates was performed within the limits of the United States from type set therein; or the lithographic or photoengraving processes used in producing the text were wholly performed within the limits of the United States, and that the printing of the text and the binding (if any) were also performed within the limits of the United States. That such typesetting, platemaking, lithographic or photoengraving process, printing, and binding were performed by the following establishments or individuals at the following addresses:
(GIVE THE NAMES AND ADDRESSES OF THE PERSONS OR ORGANIZATIONS WHO PERFORMED SUCH TYPESETTING OR PLATEMAKING OR LITHOGRAPHIC PROCESS OR PHOTOENGRAVING PROCESS OR PRINTING AND BINDING, ETC.)

Names **(X)** .... Addresses **(X)** ....

....

....
(Signature of affiant)

(Sign and notarize only on or after date given above)

PLACE
NOTARIAL SEAL
HERE

Subscribed and sworn to / affirmed before me this ....

day of ...., 19......

....
(Signature of notary)

FOR COPYRIGHT OFFICE USE ONLY	
Application and affidavit received	
Two copies received	
Fee received	
Renewal	

Certificate
Registration of a Claim to Copyright
in a published book manufactured in the United States of America

This Is To Certify that the statements set forth on this certificate have been made a part of the records of the Copyright Office. In witness whereof the seal of the Copyright Office is hereto affixed.

Register of Copyrights
United States of America

FORM A

CLASS	REGISTRATION NO.
A	DO NOT WRITE HERE

1. Copyright Claimant(s) and Address(es):

Name ....

Address ....

Name ....

Address ....

2. Title: ....
(Title of book)

....

3. Authors:

Name ....
(Legal name followed by pseudonym if latter appears on copies)
Citizenship ....
(Name of country)

Domiciled in U.S.A. Yes .... No .... Address ....

Name ....
(Legal name followed by pseudonym if latter appears on copies)
Citizenship ....
(Name of country)

Domiciled in U.S.A. Yes .... No .... Address ....

Name ....
(Legal name followed by pseudonym if latter appears on copies)
Citizenship ....
(Name of country)

Domiciled in U.S.A. Yes .... No .... Address ....

4. Date of Publication of This Edition:

....
(Month)   (Day)   (Year)

5. New Matter in This Version:

....

....

6. Book in English Previously Manufactured and Published Abroad: If all or a substantial part of the text of this edition was previously manufactured and published abroad in the English language, complete the following spaces:

Date of first publication of foreign edition ....
(Year)

Was registration for the foreign edition made in the U.S. Copyright Office? Yes .... No ....

If your answer is "Yes," give registration number ....

EXAMINER

Complete all applicable spaces on next page

312

7. Deposit account:

....

8. Send correspondence to:

Name .... Address ....

9. Send certificate to:

(Type or
print   Name   ....
name and
address) Address ....
(Number and street)

....
(City)   (State)   (ZIP code)

Information concerning copyright in books

When to Use Form A. Form A is appropriate for published books which have been manufactured in the United States.

What Is a "Book"? The term "books" covers not only material published in book form, but also pamphlets, leaflets, cards, and single pages containing text. Books include fiction, nonfiction, poetry, collections, directories, catalogs, and information in tabular form.

Unpublished Books. The law does not provide for registration of "book" material in unpublished form. Unpublished books are protected at common law against unauthorized use prior to publication.

Duration of Copyright. Statutory copyright in published books lasts for 28 years from the date of first publication, and may be renewed for a second 28-year term.

How to secure statutory copyright in a book

First: Produce Copies With Copyright Notice. Produce the work in copies by printing or other means of reproduction. To secure copyright, it is essential that the copies bear a copyright notice in the required form and position, as explained below.

Second: Publish the Work With Copyright Notice. The copyright law defines the "date of publication" as ". . . the earliest date when copies of the first authorized edition were placed on sale, sold, or publicly distributed by the proprietor of the copyright or under his authority, . . ."

Third: Register Your Copyright Claim. Promptly after publication, mail to the Register of Copyrights, Library of Congress,

Washington, D.C. 20540, two copies of the work as published with notice, an application on Form A, properly completed and notarized, and a fee of $6.

The Copyright Notice. The copyright notice for books shall appear on the title page or verso thereof, and shall consist of three elements: the word "Copyright," or the abbreviation "Copr.," or the symbol ©, accompanied by the name of the copyright owner and the year date of publication. Example: © John Doe 1970. Use of the symbol © may result in securing copyright in countries which are members of the Universal Copyright Convention.

NOTE: It is the act of publication with notice that actually secures copyright protection. If copies are published without the required notice, the right to secure copyright is lost, and cannot be restored.

Books manufactured abroad

In General. Form A is not appropriate for books which have been manufactured outside the United States.

Foreign-Language Books. Applications covering foreign-language books by foreign authors, manufactured abroad, should be submitted on Form A–B Foreign.

English-Language Books. Books in English manufactured abroad may be registered for "ad interim" copyright (Form A–B Ad Interim); or, if they are protected under the Universal Copyright Convention they are eligible for full-term registration on Form A–B Foreign:

(1) *Ad Interim Copyright.* Ad interim registration is necessary for protection in the United States unless copyright has been secured

under the Universal Copyright Convention. To secure ad interim copyright a claim must be registered within 6 months of first publication abroad. Ad interim copyright lasts for 5 years or until an American edition is published within the 5-year period and registered.

(2) *Universal Copyright Convention.* An English-language work by a foreign author first published abroad is eligible for full-term U.S. copyright if: (a) its author is a citizen or subject of a country which is a member of the Universal Copyright Convention, or the work was first published in such country, and (b) all published copies bear the copyright notice provided under the Universal Copyright Convention.

FOR COPYRIGHT OFFICE USE ONLY	
Application and affidavit received	
Two copies received	
Fee received	

T40 73 599